Meli Koch

Schöningh

EinFach
Englisch
Unterrichtsmodell

Series Editor: Hans Kröger

The King's Speech

by
Margot Adami
Alexa Kiko

edited by
Hans Kröger

Einzelarbeit

Partnerarbeit

Gruppenarbeit

Unterrichtsgespräch

Schreibauftrag

Hausaufgabe

Audio-CD

filmische Präsentation

Projekt, offene Aufgabe

kreative Aufgabe

szenisches Spiel, Rollenspiel

Vorwort

Der Titel der Reihe **EinFach Englisch** verdeutlicht Zielsetzung und Programm zugleich. Einerseits soll Schülerinnen und Schülern auf einfache Art und Weise der Zugang zu klassischen, aber auch neuen literarischen Werken und Filmen ermöglicht werden, andererseits sollen Lehrerinnen und Lehrern in der Praxis erprobte Unterrichtsmodelle angeboten werden, die die wichtigsten methodisch-didaktischen Ansätze ihres Faches Englisch abdecken. Dabei sind die Modelle direkt, ohne langes Einlesen einsetzbar und stellen Unterrichtsarbeit konkret vor. Als besonders hilfreich für die Praxis haben sich dabei folgende Aspekte erwiesen, die für die Gestaltung der Reihe wesentlich sind:

- Überblick über **Figurenkonstellation**, ggf. **Filmszenen** und **Inhalt**
- **Klausuren** mit **Erwartungshorizont**
- **Arbeitsblätter, Tafelbilder** und **Leitfragen** für den Unterricht
- **Piktogramme** als Hinweise auf **Unterrichts-** und **Arbeitsformen**

Das Prinzip der **„Components“** ermöglicht darüber hinaus den variablen Einsatz der Modelle in unterschiedlich konzipierten Unterrichtsreihen. Dabei stehen Machbarkeit und Praxisnähe stets im Vordergrund.

Das vorliegende Modell bezieht sich auf die britische Original-DVD *The King's Speech* (Momentum Pictures 2011) sowie alternativ auch die deutsche DVD-Version (Senator Home Entertainment 2011).

Sprachliche Betreuung: Ronnie Halligan

www.schoeningh-schulbuch.de
Schöningh Verlag, Jühenplatz 1–3, 33098 Paderborn

Druck 5 4 3 2 1 / Jahr 2017 16 15 14 13
Die letzte Zahl bezeichnet das Jahr dieses Druckes.

Umschlaggestaltung: Jennifer Kirchhof
Druck und Bindung: westermann druck GmbH, Braunschweig

ISBN 978-3-14-041174-5

Getting started

1. Describe the characters and their arrangement on the poster.
2. Analyse the way the characters are presented.

The King's Speech

The film 6
Contents 6
Biographical information 6
The characters 7
Die im Film verwendeten Titel 10
Scene index 10

Das Unterrichtsmodell 13
Vorüberlegungen zum Film 13
Konzeption des Unterrichtsmodells 13
Weiterführende Materialien 14

Klausuren 16

Component 1: Bertie, David and the others: characterizations 27

1.1 Pre-viewing activity: Film poster **27**
1.2 Long-term viewing-tasks **28**

Copy 1 Getting to know the characters **45**
Copy 2 Historical events **46**
Copy 3 Characterization **47**
Copy 4 Development **48**
Copy 5 Music and sound in the film and their effects **49**
Copy 6 The language of film: Selected terms for film analysis **50**

Component 2: Introducing a prince's life 52

2.1 The political system of the United Kingdom **52**
2.2 Duties of the monarch **53**
2.3 The Windsors **55**
2.4 Bertie: The Prince's Speech **55**

Copy 7 The political system of the United Kingdom **58**
Copy 8 The Role of the British Sovereign **59**
Copy 9 The Royal Family: Biographical information **60**
Copy 10 Family Tree **62**
Copy 11 The Royal Family – task **63**
Copy 12 The Royal Family – solutions **64**
Copy 13 How well do you know the Royal Family? **66**
Copy 14 Introducing a prince's life – first scene of the film **67**
Copy 15 a/b Royal life/A commoner's life **68**

Component 3: My game, my rules, my turf – speech therapy 69

3.1 Sir Blandine-Bentham: Speech therapy? **69**
3.2 Lionel Logue: Speech therapy! **70**
3.3 The history of speech therapy **74**

Copy 16 Christian Nordqvist: What is Stammering, Stuttering? **76**

Component 4: Family relations 78

4.1 Bertie and his father **78**
4.2 David and his father **79**
4.3 Bertie's childhood **81**
4.4 Wallis Simpson **83**
4.5 David and Bertie **84**

Copy 17 Bertie and his father **86**
Copy 18 Her Majesty Queen Elizabeth II **87**
Copy 19 a/b Hot Seat David/Hot Seat Bertie **88**
Copy 20 a/b Hot Seat questions to David/Hot Seat questions to Bertie **89**
Copy 21 Wallis Simpson and Bertie and David **90**

Component 5: A strange friendship 91

5.1 Bertie and Lionel **91**
5.2 Wallis and Edward **93**
5.3 Edward, Wallis and Hitler **95**
5.4 Truth & Fiction **95**

Copy 22 The King's Speech – Mock Exam **97**
Copy 23 William Butler Yeats: A Model for the Laureate (1937) **98**
Copy 24 Roger Lewis: "'That Woman: The Life of Wallis Simpson, Duchess of Windsor' by Anne Sebba" **99**
Copy 25 a/b Photo/Ein König und die Nazis **101**
Copy 26 Queen Elizabeth's posthumous endorsement of Lionel Logue **102**
Copy 27 David Freeman: "Perspective: How true is 'The King's Speech?'" **103**

Component 6: Post-viewing activities 105

6.1 The King speaks **105**
6.2 Reviews **108**
6.3 The actors and their roles **110**
6.4 The screenplay **112**
6.5 Is the monarchy still relevant? **112**

Copy 28 King George VI addresses the nation/Prime Minister Chamberlain declares war **115**
Copy 29 Hannah Pilarczyk: „Eure Majestät, Ihr stottert" **117**
Copy 30 Jack Marx Live Blog: "The critics are wrong: The King's speech s-s-sucks" **118**
Copy 31 Interview: Colin Firth Talks The King's Speech **119**
Copy 32 Actors about their roles in the film or the film **122**
Copy 33 Cartoon analysis **123**
Copy 34 The King's Speech writer Seidler: "I was writing about myself" **124**
Copy 35 Think Pair Share: Is the royal family still relevant? **125**
Copy 36 Cartoons **126**
Copy 37 Is the monarchy still relevant? Amy Shields: Yes **127**
Copy 38 Is the monarchy still relevant? Ralph Blackburn: No **128**

The film

Contents

After King Edward VIII abdicates in 1936 to marry his mistress Wallis Simpson, a divorced woman, his younger brother Albert (called "Bertie" by family and close friends) has to succeed him and becomes King George VI. Bertie, who has been suffering from a speech defect since his early childhood, seems hardly suitable for this position where he has to lead a nation on the verge of war – a nation in need of a strong king. His wife Elizabeth finds the unconventional Australian speech therapist Lionel Logue who is to help her husband master his stammer and to prepare the monarch for his public speeches and radio broadcasts. New and unheard of methods effect the first amelioration and the two very different men approach each other with respect, a relationship which evolves into an exceptional friendship. Thanks to Logue's treatment and King George's hard work the King's stammer is reduced so that, in the end, he is able to give a radio speech without any noticeable hesitation on the occasion of Britain's declaration of war against Germany in 1939.

Biographical information

David Seidler was born in London in 1937 and grew up in London, Surrey and America. During his journey with his Jewish family to the US Seidler developed a stammer. He believes that his speech impediment might have been caused by the emotional trauma of WW II. Seidler moved to Hollywood after his graduation in English at Cornell and became a writer. Because of his stammer he had always been interested in George VI's story, but the Queen mother asked Seidler not to pursue this story during her lifetime. Seidler won an Academy Award for the original screenplay of *The King's Speech*.

Colin Firth was born in Hampshire in 1960 and spent his early childhood in Africa because of his missionary grandparents. After school in Winchester Firth spent two years at the Drama Centre in Chalk Farm. He was discovered during his last term there. Then Firth started his career in a theatre play. After that he starred in several TV and cinema films. One of his most famous roles is "Mr Darcy" in BBC's version of *Pride and Prejudice*. Firth won an Academy Award for his portrayal of George VI in 2011.

In 1951 **Geoffrey Rush** was born in Queensland, Australia. At the age of 20 he started acting in a theatre play with the Queensland Theatre Company. Rush has an Arts Degree from the University of Queensland. In 1981 he started his film career but he still acted in theatre plays. With his performance in "Shine" in 1996 Rush attracted international attention and won different awards, including an Academy Award. Another very famous role is "Barbarossa" in *Pirates of the Caribbean*. Rush was nominated for an Academy Award for his performance as Lionel Logue.

Helena Bonham Carter was born in London in 1966 into a famous family. After attending school in London, Bonham Carter started her career as an actress. After a second place in a national poetry competition Bonham Carter put her photo in a casting directory. A short time later she played in a film and acted in a first commercial. Bonham Carter's most famous films are "A Room with a View" and "Harry Potter". Bonham Carter has a "domestic partnership" with Tim Burton, a well-known American director. She was nominated for an Academy Award for her performance in *The King's Speech*.

The characters

King George V

(1885–1936), actually George Frederick Ernest Albert of Saxe-Coburg and Gotha, was King of the United Kingdom and the British Dominions and Emperor of India from 1910 until his death in 1936. In 1893 he married Princess Victoria Mary of Teck (known as *Mary*). She had been engaged to his older brother who died some weeks after the formal engagement. After his brother's death George became Prince of Wales.
Together with Mary he had six children: Edward (1894–1972), *Prince of Wales*, known as "David"; Albert (1895–1952), *Duke of York*, known as "Bertie"; Maria (1897–1965), *Princess Royal*; Henry (1900–1974), *Duke of Gloucester*; George (1902–1942), *Duke of Kent*; John (1905–1919), known as "Johnny".
In the film *The King's Speech* George V, a very strict father to his children, explains to his son Albert the importance of radio broadcasts and wants him to read out the traditional Christmas broadcast, thus preparing him for public duties. The King dislikes his eldest son Edward's relationship with Wallis Simpson and feels that he has to rely on his second-born son. After quite a long illness George V dies in Sandringham and Edward becomes King.

Queen Mary

(1867–1953), Victoria Mary Augusta Louise Olga Pauline Claudine Agnes of Teck, chose Mary as her royal name in accordance with Queen Victoria's wish to be the last Queen called Victoria. She was engaged to Prince Albert Victor in 1891, but he died some weeks later. Having become close to his younger brother George during the period of mourning, she married George in 1893. They deeply loved each other until his death in 1936.
In the film *The King's Speech* she supports her eldest son Edward in his position as new King, but when he wants to marry Wallis Simpson, a divorced woman, she gives her support to Bertie.

King Edward VIII

(1894–1972), Edward Albert Christian George Andrew Patrick David, known as *David*, was the oldest son of King George V and after his father's death he became King of the United Kingdom and the Dominions of the British Commonwealth and Emperor of India. Edward's relationship with his family was clouded by his womanising and later by his affair with and love of Wallis Simpson, which finally led to his abdication only eleven months after his accession. After their marriage in 1937, Edward, who received the title *Duke of Windsor* from his brother, and Wallis mainly lived in France and in the USA.
The King's Speech covers the period of Edward's reign. Pressure from the conservative government under Prime Minister Stanley Baldwin as well as from the Anglican Church represented by Archbishop Cosmo Lang, who could not agree to Edward marrying a twice-divorced woman with two living ex-husbands, finally leads to his abdication on 11 December 1936 – making his brother Albert the new King.

King George VI

(1895–1952), Albert Frederick Arthur George, known as *Bertie*, was King George V's second son and traditionally had the title *Duke of*

York. Albert and his siblings, mainly educated by nannies, got on well with each other, but Albert and his elder brother Edward were closest. However, Albert was often mocked because of his stammer which made him try many different forms of speech therapy throughout his life. In 1923 Albert married Lady Elizabeth Bowes-Lyon. They had two daughters, Elizabeth (who is today Queen Elizabeth II) and Margaret.
The film shows Elizabeth as a loving wife supporting her husband in everything he does. After the disaster of Bertie's speech at the opening ceremony of the *British Empire Exhibition* in 1925 she finds him the Australian speech therapist Lionel Logue, who is able to help and cure Albert.

Elizabeth Bowes-Lyon (1900–2002), Queen Elizabeth, later known as *Queen Mum*, was George VI's wife and Elizabeth II's mother. She was raised in Glamis Castle in Scotland and later married Albert, after having turned him down twice. Until her death she was the most popular member of the Royal Family.
In *The King's Speech* she reassures her husband and gives him self-confidence, also by organising the speech therapy with Lionel Logue and thus helping her husband to overcome his stammer. Although she had married the second-born son and thus had never thought of becoming Queen herself, she accepts this new role and is able to convince through her strong and friendly personality.

Queen Elizabeth II (born 1926), Elizabeth Alexandra Mary, is the daughter of King George VI and Queen Elizabeth and is the current Queen of the United Kingdom of Great Britain and Northern Ireland, and of her other Realms and Territories and Head of the Commonwealth.

Wallis Simpson (1896–1986), actually Bessie Wallis Warfield, was the woman who was the reason for Kind Edward VIII's abdication in 1936. She was divorced and still married to her second husband when David/Edward fell in love with her. Thus, their relationship was highly disliked by the Royal Family.
In the film *The King's Speech* she is also said to have an affair with the German foreign minister Joachim von Ribbentrop. After her second divorce Edward wants to marry her, but the Anglican Church refuses. As a consequence Edward VIII abdicates after only eleven months on the throne. After their marriage Wallis Simpson officially became *Duchess of Windsor* but was still not accepted by Queen Mary.

Archbishop Cosmo Lang (1864–1945), William Cosmo Gordon Lang, was Archbishop of York and then of Canterbury with close ties to the Royal Family. However, when Edward wanted to marry Wallis Simpson, Lang took a strong moral stance and refused to administer the Coronation Oath.
In the film, shortly before the death of King George V, Lang is present at Sandringham, ingratiating himself with David. After the abdication crisis he does not want to lose his influential position and fights Lionel Logue's close relation with Albert.

Lionel George Logue (1880–1953) was an Australian speech therapist who had studied music and had worked as an actor, a teacher of elocution and an accountant. In 1907 he married Myrtle Gruenert in Perth and they had three sons. After World War I Logue treated Australian war veterans suffering from impaired speech. In 1924 the family moved to London where Logue set up a speech-defect practice.
In the film Elizabeth contacts Logue after one of her husband's disastrous speeches. Logue's refusal of the Royal Protocol, his unconventional methods, his lack of qualifications and his direct approach first seem to pose unsurmountable problems, but a first success convinces Albert to continue the therapy which finally leads to a friendship between the two men.

Myrtle Logue 1907 Lionel Logue married Myrtle Gruenert in Perth. They had three sons.
In the film Myrtle supports her husband and gives him advice when the interpersonal problems between Logue and the King come to a head.

Winston Churchill (1874–1965), Sir Winston Leonard Spencer-Churchill, was a famous British Conservative politician and statesman who held many different political positions such as for example Chancellor of the Exchequer or Prime Minister. He led the British people through World War II.
The King's Speech shows him as a supporter of King George VI.

Stanley Baldwin (1867–1947), 1st Earl Baldwin of Bewdley, was a British Conservative politician who served as Prime Minister three times under three different monarchs.
In the film he supports Albert on his way to the throne and wants Edward VIII to abdicate.

Die im Film verwendeten Titel

Da die meisten Schüler sich in Adelskreisen nicht besonders gut auskennen, folgt eine Auflistung der im Film verwendeten Adelstitel inklusive deutscher Übersetzung.

peerage	Adelsstand, Adelswürde
courtesy title	Ehrentitel
His Royal Highness, Her Royal Highness (HRH)	Seine, Ihre Königliche Hoheit
His Majesty, Her Majesty (HM)	Seine, Ihre Majestät
His Imperial Majesty The King Emperor	Seine Kaiserliche Hoheit (in Bezug auf Britisch-Indien)
Queen Mother, Queen Mum	Königinmutter
Queen dowager	Königswitwe, Königinwitwe
Prince of Wales	Fürst von Wales (Wales ist ein Fürstentum)
Prince Royal, Princess Royal	Kronprinz, Kronprinzessin
Duke, Duchess	Herzog, Herzogin
Prince Consort	Prinzgemahl
Grand Duke	Großherzog
Earl, Countess	britischer Graf, Gräfin
Count, Countess	Graf, Gräfin

Scene index

Based on the original UK-DVD version (*Momentum Pictures, 2011*) because it offers of the possibility of watching the film with subtitles. On the right you can find the time of the chapters of the German DVD (*Senator Home Entertainment, 2011*).

Scene	Summary	Time English DVD	Zeit deutsche DVD
Chapter 1	Bertie delivers a speech at the closing ceremony of the British Empire Exhibition at Wembley. The speech turns out to be a disaster as he stammers badly. Bertie and his wife seek help from a doctor who suggests smoking and sterilized marbles as a therapy, but Bertie does not see the sense in this and begs Elizabeth to promise him no more therapy. In the next scene Elizabeth and her driver are seen searching for an address in foggy London.	0:00:00	0:00:00
Chapter 2	Elizabeth, calling herself "Mrs Johnson", enters a building and visits Lionel Logue, an Australian speech therapist. When Lionel finds out the real name of his patient, he promises to help him if he trusts him. In the next scene Lionel tells his family about his day. In the meantime Bertie tells his two daughters a penguin story. Elizabeth talks to Bertie about the new therapist. Lionel speaks at an audition for the role as Richard III but is rejected.	0:07:44	0:07:35

Scene	Summary	Time English DVD	Zeit deutsche DVD
Chapter 3	Elizabeth and Bertie visit Lionel. During their first session Bertie and Lionel have a bet and Bertie must record his voice reading Shakespeare's *Hamlet* and listening to music at the same time. The Prince is not convinced of Lionel's strange methods, his ideas of being equal and his wanting to talk about his private life. At Christmas Bertie's father delivers a speech on the radio and reminds Bertie of the importance of the radio and his duties as a member of the Royal Family. George V predicts Edward's fall and Hitler's rise.	0:16:56	0:17:23 0:28:21 (chapter 4)
Chapter 4	Bertie is relaxing on his couch and listening to music. He finally listens to his recording and is astonished. Elizabeth enters the room. Together they visit Lionel again who now wants to have the shilling he has won. Bertie wants to start therapy immediately and needs Lionel to assist him during events. They both work hard and have meetings every day. Bertie's first speech is a success with the help of his newly gained strategies. In the next scene Bertie meets David at Sandringham Estate as the King is dying.	0:31:19	s.o.
Chapter 5	King George appears to be confused. He cannot make his own decisions and is assisted by advisers, a nurse, Archbishop Cosmo Lang, his wife and sons. During dinner Archbishop Cosmo Lang makes sure that David knows he will support him when George dies. Queen Mary congratulates David, who is now King Edward VIII. Lionel finds out that the King has died and is playing a Shakespeare role for his sons when he hears a knock at the door.	0:37:56	0:37:26
Chapter 6	Bertie visits Lionel just after his father's death. They have a drink and Bertie tells Lionel about his father's last words. Then Bertie builds a model plane because his father did not want him to do so as a child. In the meantime they talk about Bertie's childhood, his problems and his dead brother Johnny. In the next scene Elizabeth and Bertie visit David at Balmoral Castle. Wallis Simpson welcomes them, but Elizabeth does not let her have her way. David does everything to please Wallis. Bertie tries to talk to David about his worries concerning Hitler and Wallis, but David does not care. Bertie is shocked about David's idea of marrying Wallis. They have an argument and Bertie starts stammering again.	0:45:16	0:44:47 0:54:03 (chapter 7)
Chapter 7	Bertie tells Lionel about his communication problems with regard to David. Lionel finds out that Bertie does not stammer when he swears. They go for a walk in the park. Lionel tries to make Bertie want to become the next King, and Bertie does not want to listen, and insults him and stops his lessons immediately. In the next scene Prime Minister Baldwin tells Bertie that the King cannot marry a divorced woman and that Wallis Simpson has other lovers apart from Edward VIII. Lionel tells Myrtle about his problems with a patient and she advises him to apologize, but Bertie refuses to see Lionel. Winston Churchill tells Bertie that his brother's marriage will not be accepted and that Britain needs a monarch the country can stand behind, united. Furthermore, Churchill suggests another possibility. David tells Bertie that he must marry Wallis.	0:58:12	

Scene	Summary	Time English DVD	Zeit deutsche DVD
Chapter 8	David abdicates and Bertie becomes King George VI, has to give his first official address to some politicians, and stammers again. Elizabeth and her daughters prepare their move to Buckingham Palace. Elizabeth reassures Bertie when he has doubts concerning his Christmas broadcast and the coronation. Elizabeth and Bertie visit Lionel at his home as Bertie wants to apologize and finally give Lionel his shilling. Lionel also apologizes. Myrtle is shocked when she finds the King and Queen in her flat.	1:07:04	1:02:33 1:13:53 (chapter 9)
Chapter 9	Lionel and Bertie inspect Westminster Abbey, the place of the coronation. Archbishop Cosmo Lang is very surprised to meet Bertie's speech therapist, who is supposed to sit in the King's box during the coronation ceremony. Bertie does not want to rehearse but confronts Lionel with his lack of expertise and qualifications. Lionel insists on the fact that he never pretended to be a doctor and that there was no training in the past in Australia. Archbishop Lang advises Bertie to do without Lionel but Bertie stands by Lionel and rehearses the coronation.	1:17:52	s.o.
Chapter 10	Archbishop Lang, Bertie, Elizabeth and the two daughters watch the coronation film the archbishop has produced. After that they watch a news report on Hitler and the Nazis in Germany. Prime Minister Baldwin tells Bertie about his resignation. Neville Chamberlain takes his place as Prime Minister, as Baldwin was obviously wrong about Hitler's intentions.	1:27:07	1:27:35
Chapter 11	Bertie meets Archbishop Lang, Prime Minister Chamberlain and Winston Churchill. Churchill admits that he had a speech impediment, too. Bertie enters the recording room, which has been redecorated, and delivers his speech successfully. Lionel stays in the room and is thanked for his support. His audience at Buckingham Palace congratulate Bertie on his first war-time speech. In the final scene the Royal Family presents itself on the balcony.	1:34:21	1:34:49
Chapter 12	end titles	1:47:16	1:47:45

Das Unterrichtsmodell

Vorüberlegungen zum Film

Filmanalyse ist aus dem Englischunterricht nicht mehr wegzudenken. Zum einen ist die Analyse mehrfach kodierter Texte im Oberstufenunterricht in Englisch in den Richtlinien vorgegeben und ist auch in Klausuren obligatorisch, zum anderen lösen Medien der Moderne bei den heutigen Schülern ein großes Interesse aus, da diese in der heutigen, von zahlreichen Medien beeinflussten Welt das Medium Film sowohl zur Information als auch zum Vergnügen häufig nutzen. Um die Reflexionsfähigkeit der Schüler zu trainieren, ist es besonders wichtig, Filme auch im Unterricht einzusetzen und vor allem zu analysieren, um den Schülern die Fähigkeit zur Dekodierung filmischer Mittel und deren Wirkungsweise zu vermitteln. Darüber hinaus können sich die Schüler im Unterricht über ihre Filmeindrücke und privaten Sehgewohnheiten austauschen und ihren Erfahrungsschatz erweitern.
Der mit vier Oscars und sieben BAFTAs ausgezeichnete Film *The King's Speech* des britischen Regisseurs Tom Hooper eignet sich aus verschiedenen Gründen für den Einsatz im Englischunterricht der Oberstufe hervorragend:
Der Film *The King's Speech* bietet zahlreiche Ansätze zur Filmanalyse, da viele filmische Stilmittel verwendet werden, die den Schülern in der Analyse aufschlussreiche Einsichten in die Arbeit mit audiovisuellen Medien ermöglichen (wie z. B. *cross-cutting*, der Einsatz von Filmmusik und anderen Geräuschen sowie interessante *settings* und eine anregende Kameraführung).
Der cineastisch anspruchsvolle Film fügt sich ideal in das Oberthema *British History* ein, da er Einblicke in das Leben der britischen Königsfamilie ermöglicht, aber auch die Herausforderungen darstellt, die ein royales Leben mit sich bringt. Ferner werden die Veränderungen in der Rolle eines Königs im 20. Jahrhundert porträtiert. Das sonst eher schülerferne Thema *Monarchy* wird den Schülern in diesem Film auf besonders feinfühlige Art nahegebracht, sodass sie sich in die Situation von Bertie sehr gut einfühlen können.
Sprachlich ist der Film durch das gehobene Sprachregister, das von den Mitgliedern der Royal Family verwendet wird, als anspruchsvoll, aber durch die (bereits thematisch vorausgesetzte) klare Aussprache der Charaktere gut verständlich einzuordnen. Beim Einsatz des Films in einem Grundkurs lässt sich das Verständnis durch die Möglichkeit englischer Untertitel bei der britischen DVD vereinfachen.
Bei der politischen Rede handelt es sich um eine für den oberstufengerechten Englischunterricht obligatorische Textsorte. Es liegt also nahe, die Originalreden George VI, die im Film dargestellt sind, über den Einsatz des Filmes hinaus im Unterricht zu besprechen und zu analysieren.
Auch über die Film- und Textanalyse hinaus bietet *The King's Speech* im Hinblick auf interkulturelles Lernen und die britische Geschichte, aber auch hinsichtlich familiärer Beziehungen und Konflikte sowie des Themas Freundschaft zahlreiche Möglichkeiten für produktions- und handlungsorientierte Aufgabenstellungen.

Konzeption des Unterrichtsmodells

Das Unterrichtsmodell gliedert sich in sechs *Components* mit verschiedenen inhaltlichen Schwerpunkten, die nach einer ersten Thematisierung der Hintergründe der Chronologie des Films folgen.

Component 1, „Bertie, David and the others: characterizations", bezieht sich vor allem auf *long-term viewing-tasks*, die von den Schülerinnen und Schülern weitgehend selbstständig

während der Behandlung des Films bearbeitet werden sollen. Hier werden die verschiedenen Charaktere detailliert und in ihrer Entwicklung analysiert.
In ***Component 2***, „Introducing a prince's life", werden die verschiedenen historischen Persönlichkeiten hinter den Charakteren des Films näher beleuchtet. Darüber hinaus werden Strukturen des politischen Systems in Großbritannien allgemein sowie Besonderheiten der Rolle des britischen Monarchen thematisiert. Filmisch werden hier die ersten Szenen des Films analysiert sowie ein ausgewählter Ausschnitt aus dem weiteren Verlauf, der den Schülerinnen und Schülern jedoch ohne weiteren Kontext verständlich ist.
Component 3 behandelt das Thema der *speech defects* und *speech therapy*. Neben den inhaltlichen Aspekten liegt hier ein weiterer Schwerpunkt auf der Einübung einzelner *skills*. Die thematisierten Filmszenen schließen sich direkt an die in *Component 2* behandelten an.
In ***Component 4*** geht es um das Thema der komplexen Familienbeziehung in Berties Verwandtschaft, von denen im folgenden ***Component 5*** weiterführend verschiedene Aspekte von ungewöhnlichen Freundschaften betrachtet werden. Hier findet sich auch ein Vorschlag für eine Probeklausur.
Component 6 beinhaltet *post-viewing tasks* zu Rezensionen und weiterführendem Material.

Weiterführende Materialien

Literatur:
- Lutz Walther (ed.): The King's Speech. The Shooting Script by David Seidler. Stuttgart, Reclam, 2012.
- Marc Logue and Peter Conradi: The King's Speech. How One Man Saved The British Monarchy. London, Quercus, 2010.

BBC:
- Edward VIII:
  http://www.bbc.co.uk/archive/edward_viii/12923.shtml
- Winston Churchill:
  http://www.bbc.co.uk/history/people/winston_churchill
- Wallis Simpson:
  http://www.bbc.co.uk/news/uk-13112678
  http://news.bbc.co.uk/2/hi/programmes/world_news_america/9368544.stm
  http://www.bbc.co.uk/news/entertainment-arts-14770900
- Queen Elizabeth, The Queen Mother:
  http://news.bbc.co.uk/hi/english/static/obituaries/queen_mother/
  http://www.bbc.co.uk/archive/ww2outbreak/7930.shtml
- Lionel Logue:
  http://www.bbc.co.uk/news/entertainment-arts-12116320
  http://news.bbc.co.uk/local/leicester/hi/people_and_places/history/newsid_9377000/9377098.stm
- George VI:
  http://www.bbc.co.uk/archive/ww2outbreak/7918.shtml
  http://www.bbc.co.uk/history/historic_figures/george_vi_king.shtml
- CD: "A King's Speech. The Radio 4 play by MARK BURGESS".

Biographien:
- Sarah Bradford: George VI. London, Penguin, 2011.
- Taylor Darbyshire: King George VI. An Intimate and Authoritative Life of the King by one who has had special facilities, and first published with the approval of His Majesty when Duke of York. London, Hutchinson & Co., 1937.

- Sebastian Haffner: Winston Churchill. Mit Selbstzeugnissen und Bilddokumentationen. Reinbek, Rowohlt, 2002.
- Anne Sebba: That Woman. The Life of Wallis Simpson, Duchess of Windsor. London, Phoenix, 2012.
- William Shawcross: Queen Elizabeth The Queen Mother. Oxford, Macmillan, 2009.

Internet:

- Special Release – The Coronation of King George VI, 1937/05/18 (1937): http://archive.org/details/1937-05-18_The_Coronation_of_King_George_VI
- Audio of King George VI's Sept. 3, 1939 speech: www.youtube.com/watch?v=DAhFW_auT20
- King George's Christmas broadcast 1939: http://archives.cbc.ca/society/monarchy/clips/12704/
- Profiles on Edward VIII, Queen Elizabeth, Wallis Simpson, King George VIII, Stanley Baldwin: http://news.bbc.co.uk/2/hi/uk_news/2689033.stm
- Speech Therapy:
  http://www.rcslt.org/
  http://www.speechtherapy.co.uk/
  http://www.nhscareers.nhs.uk/details/default.aspx?id=288
- Winston Churchill:
  http://www.winstonchurchill.org/

Filme:

- W./E. Studiocanal, 2012.
- Die Queen. Concorde Video, 2007.
- King George VI – Der Mann hinter "The King's Speech". Schröder Media Handels GmbH, 2011.
- Edward & Mrs Simpson. Network, 2005.
- Wallis & Edward. Acorn Media, 2006.
- Winston Churchill – The Man behind the Myth. IMC Vision, 2005.
- Gathering Storm. Warner Home Video, 2003.

Klausuren

Im Folgenden finden sich zwei Klausuren sowie ein Text für eine mündliche Prüfung. Die erste Klausur lässt sich während der Bearbeitung des Unterrichtsmodells, aber auch im Anschluss daran sowohl in einem Grund- als auch Leistungskurs einsetzen. Nach Bearbeitung des Unterrichtmodells bieten sich der Einsatz der zweiten Klausur, die eher für einen Grundkurs geeignet ist, sowie die mündliche Prüfung an.

Klausur 1 bezieht sich auf die zweite und die folgenden Therapiesitzungen von Lionel und Bertie. Nachdem in der ersten Sitzung nur gesprochen wurde und lediglich Berties Stimme auf Schallplatte aufgenommen wurde, wird in dieser Szene, die sich an eine Auseinandersetzung zwischen Bertie und seinem Vater auf Schloss Sandringham anschließt, unbeirrt gearbeitet. Man sieht Lionels außergewöhnliche Methoden und das Vertrauen, das Bertie in seinen Sprachtherapeuten setzt, aber in der durch *cross-cutting* eingebetteten Rede Berties in einer Fabrik auch seine „kleinen" Erfolge. Die Aufgaben in der Klausur sehen eine inhaltliche Auseinandersetzung mit der *film review* Alison McCulloughs und des Films *The King's Speech* vor, sowie eine Analyse der filmischen Mittel, die Hooper verwendet, um Logues unorthodoxe Methoden zum einen und das Vertrauen zwischen Patient und Therapeut zum anderen darzustellen. In Aufgabe 3 können die Schüler zwischen einem Kommentar und einer kreativen Aufgabe auswählen. Beides wurde schon in *Component 5* geübt. Es empfiehlt sich also, den Film ganz bzw. einschließlich des Streits zwischen Lionel und Bertie gezeigt zu haben, um die Analyse filmischer Mittel ausreichend vorbereitet zu haben. Für die Lösung der kreativen Aufgabe muss die Therapiesitzung nach dem Tod von George V besprochen worden sein.

Klausur 2 bezieht sich auf die letzte Rede, die Bertie im Film hält. Nachdem Lionel mit ihm im Buckingham Palace geübt hat, hält Bertie eine Rede an die Nation, in der es um die Kriegserklärung Großbritanniens an Deutschland geht. Da die Rede in dieser Krise eine extrem große Bedeutung hat, ist Bertie sehr nervös, meistert den Text mit Lionels Hilfe jedoch bravourös. Der Klausur liegt auch ein Text zugrunde, in dem der Herausgeber der „GQ" Dylan Jones erklärt, wie er seinen Sprachfehler überwunden hat. In der ersten Aufgabe müssen die Schüler herausstellen, wie Jones dies geschafft hat. In der zweiten Aufgabe werden die Stilmittel untersucht, die Hooper verwendet, um zu zeigen, wie Bertie sein Stottern überwindet. In Aufgabe 3 können sich die Schüler zwischen einem Dankesschreiben an Lionel und einem Kommentar entscheiden. Beides wurde bereits in *Component 5* trainiert.

Das Gedicht bietet sich aufgrund seiner Kürze und Klarheit als Text für eine **mündliche Prüfung** an. Das Thema *friendship* wird in *Component 5* behandelt, so dass die Schülerinnen und Schüler im Anschluss diverse Beispiele für den in der dritten Aufgabe geforderten Filmbezug liefern können.

The King's Speech (film analysis)

I. film scene: The King's Speech, directed by Tom Hooper, 2010; 0:35:09 – 0:37:25 (German DVD) / 0:34:40 – 0:36:56 (British DVD)

II. source of the text: http://www.rcslt.org/giving_voice/news/ks_review [12 02 2013]
Alison McCullough, 2010

(...) Written by David Seidler, who himself suffered from a stammer, The King's Speech is more than just another British costume drama. It is a surprisingly emotional film that explores the pain, anguish and anxiety of a stammerer focussing on a lesser-known piece of pre-war British history.
The film traces the therapeutic relationship between Prince Albert (Colin Firth) and an unconventional speech therapist named Lionel Logue (Geoffrey Rush), who helped him deal with a crippling stammer as he eventually assumed the throne – as George VI. George VI (called Bertie by family) and his supportive wife Elizabeth, played wonderfully by Helena Bonham Carter, had tried everything – including getting the prince to enunciate with a mouth full of marbles, in a scene reminiscent of Pygmalion.
Bertie has all but given up until Elizabeth finds the extraordinary Lionel Logue, played by Geoffrey Rush, an Australian speech therapist who promises to succeed where all others had failed.
This film portrays the impact that communication disability can have upon a man's life whether he is a prince or pauper. At a time when the Royal Family is forced to engage more with the public – as radio becomes more and more popular – it is clear that if Bertie is to take the throne he must master his stammer. As his wife Elizabeth points out he has no choice but to stay in his present job.
Colin Firth's sensitive portrayal of King George VI is simply outstanding. He shows how the communication disability affects all aspects of the sufferer's life. He brought out all the frustration, embarrassment, self-doubt and often anger associated with this disability.
Logue, an unorthodox therapist and frustrated actor takes on the Prince but refuses to treat him any differently to his other patients. He demonstrates the power and importance of the therapeutic relationship in dealing with this crippling communication difficulty and insists on being the King's equal in the relationship. Alongside being his therapist the film also shows the development of a mature friendship with the prince's 'commoner' speech therapist becoming his first real 'friend'.
The techniques used in the film develop the King's confidence by dealing with the psychological barriers to his fluency as well as the physical techniques to improve fluent flowing speech. Whilst some of the unorthodox methods in the film appear extreme to what would be considered normal practice today they still address these two focuses for therapy which are still relevant. The intimacy and trust between the client and therapist demonstrated so beautifully is absolutely crucial to the success of the intervention for anyone working with communication disability.
(...) At first glance the story of a royal overcoming a speech impediment might not seem like gripping cinema – but with the fabulous script and wonderful performances of Colin Firth, Geoffrey Rush and Helena Bonham Carter the film is much more than just about a stammer – it is passionate, heartbreaking and uplifting and is one of the most engaging films I have seen in years.

Alison McCullough is the County Policy Officer at the Royal College of Speech and Language Therapists (RCSLT) which was established on 6 January 1945 to promote the art and science of speech and language therapy – the care for individuals with communication, swallowing, eating and drinking difficulties.

Pygmalion George Bernard Shaw wrote a play entitled "Pygmalion". In Shaw's play, a poor girl is trained how to speak properly in order pass as a duchess at a party.
pauper a poor person

engaging *here:* fascinating, enchanting – *bezaubernd*

Assignments

1. State the aspects of "The King's Speech" which are critically assessed by the reviewer and present examples from the film to prove these statements. (comprehension)
2. Watch the scenes in Lionel's practice and at one of Bertie's speeches. Analyse the way Lionel's "unorthodox" methods are presented with the help of cinematic devices and examine the "intimacy and trust between the client and patient [that are] demonstrated so beautifully". (analysis)
3. Choose between the following two tasks:
   a) Write a comment on McCullough's statement that "The King's Speech" is "passionate, heartbreaking and uplifting (…)" and even "one of the most engaging films" she has seen in years. (comment)
   b) In the role of Bertie write a letter to Lionel after the speech you delivered in the film extract in which you refer to the problems you were having as a child and what happened to you on the day of the speech. (re-creation of text)
   (**note**: the film does not tell us which year it is, but it's about 1935. At that point in time Bertie and Elizabeth and their two daughters lived at their London residence, 145 Piccadilly)

Erwartungshorizont zu Klausur 1

Zu 1:

- more than a costume drama (l. 2); evidence: deals with friendship and problems of a royal, not just with court life
- surprisingly emotional (l. 2); evidence: prince talks about problems, feelings and childhood, you can tune into the character perfectly
- Elizabeth played wonderfully by Helena Bonham Carter (ll. 8f.); evidence: convincing, e.g. scene with the doctor
- Colin Firth outstanding (l. 19); evidence: stammer seems natural and real
- brings out all the frustration, embarrassment, self-doubt and often anger associated with this disability (ll. 20ff.); evidence: outbreaks of anger convincing, convincing when he cries and tells E. that he is just a naval officer
- Unorthodox therapist (l. 23) / unorthodox methods (l. 31), rolling around the floor; evidence: "Up comes Royal Highness, down comes her Royal Highness"
- demonstrates the power and importance of the therapeutic relationship (l. 25); intimacy and trust between client and therapist demonstrated so beautifully (ll. 33f.); evidence: all scenes in Lionel's practice but the first one
- fabulous script (l. 37), funny (when he screams swear words) and no superfluous scenes
- wonderful performance by Geoffrey Rush (l. 38); evidence: funny and convincing

Zu 2:

- Bertie trusts him because he joins in every activity Lionel asks him to join in; as ridiculous as it might seem
- scene begins with a strange sound which is only then shown to come from Bertie and Logue: camera zooms out on the two men who are standing face to face and seem to be equal
- camera zooms in on the faces and past the faces to the sofa: they have left behind the stage of Bertie's passivity
- camera zooms out again, Bertie is lying on the floor, Lionel is kneeling in front of him, an open book, glasses etc. are on the floor around them: atmosphere of intensive work
  Logue touches him: physical contact shows intimacy and trust
- cross cutting!: background music leads over to the speech and in a moment of hesitation in the speech Logue's voice is heard as if in Bertie's head, but in fact it leads back to the next therapy scene; "M" sound of "mother" in the therapy leads to "manufacturing" in the speech while Logue's voice is heard ("off"); movement of feet in therapy and during the speech
- medium shots on Bertie, Lionel and Elizabeth; to show both body language and facial expressions which express trust and a close relationship; close-ups of the faces (point of view shot from Elizabeth's perspective on Bertie's face): smiling and relaxed
- close-ups on sceptical audience to show that the average people do not believe in the success of the therapy as Bertie is still having problems; opposed by/interspersed with examples (flashbacks?) from the therapy where he can use his voice
- medium shot on Bertie on the sofa when he wants to light a cigarette, hair in disarray to show how much physical effort he puts into the therapy, but Logue forbids him to smoke and asks him to continue working ("Bertie, come on!") – which Bertie does: intimacy and friendship
- Elizabeth, Bertie and Logue seen from behind standing in front of an open window: unity, cooperation; reverse-angle shot because this impression is re-

vealed more clearly by the look on their faces, Elizabeth's stop-watch, etc., cut to an annoyed neighbour shows how strangely the therapy is perceived – and how little they care

- zoom in on Bertie's face and extreme close up of his mouth trying to articulate the word "father": link to the following scene (foreshadowing?)
- handheld camera → to show actions; to underline how hard and strange therapy is
- lively classical music: underlines active, positive atmosphere

Zu 3: a) Comment:
The students' answers will vary here. However, the structure of the comment is very important, including an introductory statement, arguments for and against, examples for every argument and a brief summary and conclusion.

b) Letter:

- **Address** (Dear Lionel, date)
- **Beginning** of the letter: For example
  - Thanks/Reference to another letter
  - Reference to last session/meeting
  - I've practised your techniques
  - practised tongue twisters
  - exercised a lot, etc.
- **Day of the speech:** For examle
  - applied all your ideas/rules
  - speech was a success
  - hesitated sometimes but your therapy helped me
  - much better than last speech
  - …
- **Childhood:** For Example
  - teased by everyone
  - difficult because parents were not very caring
  - was left with personnel
  - no friends
  - knock-knees
  - stammer
  - laughed at
  - sad when brother died
  - …
- **Conclusion** of the letter: For example
  - looking forward to seeing you
  - keep in touch
  - drop me a line
  - thank you
- **Finishing:** For example
  - best wishes
  - Albert

The King's Speech (film analysis)

I. film scene: The King's Speech, directed by Tom Hooper, 2010; 1:38:39–1:42:59 (British DVD)/ 1:38:40–1:43:31 (German DVD)

II. source of the text: http://www.stammering.org/djones.html [12 02 2013]

Speaking Out – The rules for mastering a stammer

DJ: [...] The biggest problem for me throughout my entire life, but particularly through my adult career, was introducing myself on the telephone. It undermines you if you're trying, as we often have to in our business, to be quite aggressive and over-confident. If I get tired or nervous, if I'm in a situation where I'm out of my comfort zone, it comes back instantly. But having to talk, having to sell a magazine, having to be a figurehead in a room full of people who need you to impress them – I think that has helped to eradicate it. I think practice, if you've got a certain kind of stammer, can help enormously – but it was more of a psychological thing for me – thinking, 'I can change this – there's no reason why I have to put up with it'. A lot is to do with confidence. I'm fairly certain that one of the reasons I've mastered the stammer, more than previously, is because over the past seven or eight years I have found myself doing quite a lot of public speaking – something I used to avoid. I would have had no interest before, because I had no confidence in doing it. Although I still stammer in the process, I have the confidence now. I don't mind getting up in front of 50 people or 500 people.

You have to develop a kind of arrogance. I tell my staff or people who aren't used to public speaking, to imagine that you're about to give a Best Man Speech. When you give a Best Man Speech, everybody wants everything to be great – everyone is on your side. (...)

This has probably been the best therapy I've had. I can see that it has helped me incredibly – because if you go up there, no-one's interested in your frame of mind, where you come from – but you're talking to them and they want to be entertained and informed and it's your job to do it. I think that has probably been the most important part of the whole process.

JA: What was the impact of stammering on your school years?

DJ: Well, it's not like having a debilitating disease – but it totally affected my relationships with people. We were in the forces and moved every year or 18 months, so you were constantly having to make new friends. You end up becoming monosyllabic and not talking to people and building walls around yourself. (...)

JA: Were you stammering a lot?

DJ: I was stammering very badly. There were words I just wouldn't attempt because I knew I wouldn't be able to say them without faltering, which again changes the way you behave – not just with your peers, but with teachers – everyone really. You go for the safest option – you become very internalised (if that's the right word).

Dylan Jones (DJ) is editor of GQ and author of Mr Jones' Rules, Hodder and Stoughton, 2006.
JA is Jan Andersen.
From the Spring 2007 issue of 'Speaking Out', pages 6–7.

http://www.stammering.org/djones.html

figurehead: a front man – *Galionsfigur, Aushängeschild*

debilitating: *hemmend*

forces: army

monosyllabic: *einsilbig (fig.)*

faltering: *Zögern*

internalised: withdrawn – *ruhig und in sich gekehrt*

Speaking Out: British Stammering Association's quarterly magazine

Assignments

1. Sum up the rules of "mastering a stammer" mentioned in the interview above. (comprehension)
2. Analyse the cinematic devices Hooper uses to show that Bertie has "mastered his stammer" in his last speech. (analysis)
3. Choose between the following two tasks:
   a) Write a comment on Dylan Jones's statement that one of the reasons why he has "mastered" his speech impediment "is because over the past seven or eight years [he has] found [himself] doing quite a lot of public speaking." (comment)
   b) In the role of Bertie write a letter to Lionel after the speech you delivered in the film extract in which you refer to the problems you were having as a child and what happened to you on the day of the speech. (re-creation of text)

Erwartungshorizont zu Klausur 2

Zu 1:

- having to talk, having to sell a magazine, having to be a figurehead in a room full of people who need you to impress them – I think that has helped to eradicate it (ll. 5 ff.)
- practice (l. 7)
- thinking "I can change this – there's no reason why I have to put up with it" (l. 9)
- confidence (l. 10)
- quite a lot of public speaking (l. 12)
- develop a kind of arrogance (l. 16)

Zu 2:

- close-ups on Bertie at the beginning to show his concentration and tension
- camera switches to medium shot of Lionel who supports Bertie with tips, in the course of the scene as Bertie gains more confidence the switches to Lionel become less
- switch to medium shot of Elizabeth who is concentrating on Bertie's words and seems really tense
- many switches to concentrated listeners, technicians, people at Buckingham Palace, pub crowd, Myrtle and the boys at Lionel's home, factory workers, personnel at Buckingham Palace, gentlemen's club, Bertie's smiling mother; British soldiers, crowd in front of Buckingham Palace, Archbishop Cosmo Lang, Winston Churchill
- camera angle: at the beginning high-angle shot of Bertie, then eye-level, and as he gains confidence, low-angle shots of Bertie
- classical, quiet music becomes both louder and accompanied by different instruments as Bertie speaks more fluently
- Lionel is shown nodding
- echo is used when crowd in front of Buckingham Palace is shown/reference to first speech at Empire Exhibition
- Elizabeth sighs to show relief as speech goes off perfectly well

Zu 3:

a) Comment:
The students' answers will vary here. However, the structure of the comment is very important, including an introductory statement, arguments for and against, examples for every argument and a brief summary and conclusion.

b) Letter:

- **Address** (Dear Lionel, date)
- **Beginning** of the letter: For example
  - Thanks/Reference to another letter
  - Reference to last session/meeting
  - I've practised your techniques
  - practised tongue twisters
  - exercised a lot, etc.
- **Day of the speech:** For example
  - applied all your ideas/rules
  - speech was a success
  - hesitated sometimes but your therapy helped me
  - much better than last speech
  - …

- **Childhood:** For example
  - teased by everyone
  - difficult because parents were not very caring
  - was left with personnel
  - no friends
  - knock-knees
  - stammer
  - laughed at
  - sad when brother died
  - ...
- **Conclusion** of the letter: For example
  - looking forward to seeing you
  - keep in touch
  - drop me a line
  - thank you
- **Finishing**: For example
  - best wishes

signature: Albert

Be a Friend by Edgar A. Guest

Be a friend. You don't need money:
Just a disposition sunny;
Just the wish to help another
Get along some way or other;
Just a kindly hand extended
Out to one who's unbefriended;
Just the will to give or lend,
This will make you someone's friend.

Be a friend. You don't need glory.
Friendship is a simple story.
Pass by trifling errors blindly,
Gaze on honest effort kindly,
Cheer the youth who's bravely trying,
Pity him who's sadly sighing;
Just a little labor spend
On the duties of a friend.

Be a friend. The pay is bigger
(Though not written by a figure)
Than is earned by people clever
In what's merely self-endeavor.
You'll have friends instead of neighbors
For the profits of your labors;
You'll be richer in the end
Than a prince, if you're a friend.

Collected Verse of Edgar A. Guest, The Reilly & Lee Co., Chicago,1934, p. 56

Assignments

1. Sum up what the poem is about.
2. Analyse the poem.
3. Comment on the statement "You'll be richer in the end than a prince" (l. 23f.) and refer to scenes from the film "The King's Speech".

Erwartungshorizont zur mündlichen Prüfung

Zu 1: The poem deals with friendship and what constitutes friendship. The first stanza describes how you can become someone's friend, the second stanza deals with how easy friendship is, the third stanza deals with what you get in the end for being a friend.

Zu 2: The author wants to show that friendship is simple and that in the end it pays off to be a friend.

The poem consists of three stanzas; the rhyme scheme is aa bb cc dd; ee ff gg dd; hh ii jj dd.

The keyword "friend" is repeated seven times to show both how easy and how profitable friendship is. To further underline the simplicity of friendship the image "hand" is used in line 5 to show that you just have to stretch your hand out to someone lonely in order to find a friend. Furthermore, the alliteration "simple story" in l. 10 underlines the author's intention.

The third stanza deals with what you get for being a friend. Words connoted with work are used, eg. "pay" l. 17, "figure" l. 18, "earned" l. 19, "profits" l. 22, "labors" l. 22. The last two lines consist of a comparison with a prince (ll.23f.) in order to show that friendship is more important as you gain more than money can buy.

To stress his statements and in order to make the poem sound better several alliterations are used, e.g. l. 10, l. 14, l. 15.

Zu 3: individual solutions

Component 1

Bertie, David and the others: characterizations

1.1 Pre-viewing activity: Film poster

Zur Motivation der Schüler bietet sich als Einstieg in die Unterrichtseinheit zu *The King's Speech* eine *pre-viewing activity* an. Hierzu eignet sich besonders das Filmposter.
(S. Getting started, S. 3; im Original: http://www.impawards.com/2010/posters/kings_speech.jpg)
Mithilfe dieses Plakats lernen die Schüler bereits die Hauptpersonen des Films kennen und sollen hierbei die Charaktere und ihr Arrangement beschreiben. In einem zweiten Schritt sollen sie, vor allem die Schüler eines Leistungskurses, die Art, in der die Charaktere präsentiert sind, analysieren.
Die folgenden Impulse dienen dem *warming-up*:

1. Describe the characters and their arrangement on the poster:
   - the man in the front looks serious
   - the woman is smiling, seems sophisticated and to be living in the 1920s because of her hairdo
   - the man on the right seems sympathetic and funny
   - as the earnest man is in the front this must be the king, the woman behind is the Queen and the other guy must be the man who could save him

2. Analyse the way the characters are presented:
   - as the king is the most important person in the country he is positioned in the front of the picture; his stern look shows that he is having a problem
   - the Queen looks very friendly and refined because of her clothes and her pearl earrings and necklace. As she is standing behind the King's back one can guess that she is very supportive and tries to help him in every possible way.
   - the speech therapist is presented with a suit, so he seems to be serious, too, but his facial expression makes him appear both smart and humorous

Ein alternativer Einstieg wäre ein *Brainstorming*, bei dem die Schüler formulieren, worum es in dem Film gehen könnte und welche Erwartungen sie an den Film haben.
Mögliche Fragestellungen wären hier:

What could the film be about?
Who can these people be?
What do you expect from the film?

Von diesem Einstieg ist jedoch abzuraten, wenn viele Schüler den Film bereits kennen.

Eine weitere Möglichkeit, die Behandlung von *The King's Speech* zu beginnen, bietet die offizielle Homepage des Films (http://www.kingsspeech.com/cast.html). Hier sind unter *cast* alle

Schauspieler aufgeführt, so dass die Schülerinnen und Schüler sich durch die verschiedenen Biografien sowie durch Verweise auf zahlreiche andere Filme diesem Werk nähern können.

Look at the official homepage of the film and at the cast. Use the Internet to find out more about the roles the actors mentioned here played in the past.

Zu einem späteren Zeitpunkt kann diese Internetseite noch einmal herangezogen werden, um die Rolle sowie die schauspielerische Leistung der jeweiligen Personen in diesem Film zu bewerten.

Use this Internet site to write a short assessment of the characters in the film. (s. ***Component 6, Copy 31*** und ***32***)

1.2 Long-term viewing-tasks

Um sicherzustellen, dass der Gesamteindruck des Films während der Analyse einzelner Szenen nicht verloren geht, besteht einerseits die Möglichkeit, den gesamten Film vor der Behandlung zu zeigen. Andererseits gibt es darüber hinaus noch die Option, *long-term viewing-tasks* einzusetzen, die arbeitsteilig, je nach Größe der Lerngruppe, verteilt werden können und die unabhängig von den weiteren Aufgaben während des abschnittsweisen Sehens zu bearbeiten sind.
Copy 1 "Getting to know the characters" bietet sich als Einzelarbeit an, während die folgenden sechs Aufgaben (***Copies 2–5***) arbeitsteilig, je nach Interesse der Schüler, von sechs verschiedenen Gruppen bearbeitet werden könnten: Charakterisierungen zweier Hauptcharaktere, Entwicklung zweier besonders relevanter Charaktere sowie der Einsatz und die Wirkung der Filmmusik und der historische Hintergrund zum Film.
(Falls in dem Unterricht ein besonderer Schwerpunkt auf die Behandlung der Filmmusik gelegt werden soll, bieten sich die CD mit dem Originalsoundtrack sowie der Artikel von Alexandre Desplat an, der unter http://moviemusicuk.us/2010/12/14/the-kings-speech-alexandre-desplat/ zu finden ist.)

1. Getting to know the characters (***Copy 1***)
2. Historical events (***Copy 2***)
3. Characterization of Elizabeth (***Copy 3***)
4. Characterization of Lionel (***Copy 3***)
5. Development of Bertie's character (***Copy 4***)
6. Development of David's character (***Copy 4***)
7. Music and sound in the film and their effects (***Copy 5***)

Lösungsvorschlag zu *Copy 1:*

- You needn't be governed by fear. – Lionel Logue
- And we need a king who we can all stand behind united. – Churchill
- Your services are no longer required. – Archbishop Cosmo Lang
- It was a relief knowing I wouldn't be king. – "Bertie"
- Perhaps he doesn't want to be great. – Myrtle Logue
- I have found it impossible to carry the heavy burden of responsibility. –"David"
- She calls me the fat Scottish cook. – Elizabeth
- None of this unpleasantness would be tolerated. – Queen Mary
- And the King, as Head of the Church of England, cannot marry a divorced woman. – Prime Minister Baldwin

- Oh, how lovely to see you both. – Wallis Simpson
- We've become actors. – King George V

Lösungsvorschlag zu *Copy 2:*

a) **Saturday 31 October 1925:** British Empire Exhibition: Prince Albert (the Duke of York) tries to deliver a speech at the close of the Empire Exhibition at Wembley Stadium, London, England, but is only able to stammer.
Tuesday 25 December 1934: Royal Christmas Message: King George V delivers a speech over the radio and tells this son how important the new medium is. "Bertie" tries to read the text, too, but stammers again and is bullied by his father.
Monday 20 January 1936: King George V dies at Sandringham Castle and his son "David" accedes to the throne and becomes King Edward VIII.
Friday 11 December 1936: King Edward VIII abdicates as he intends to marry Wallis Simpson, a twice-divorced American socialite and his brother "Bertie" accedes to the throne and becomes King George VI.
Wednesday 12 May 1937: King George VI is crowned at Westminster Abbey.
Sunday 3 September 1939: Prime Minister Neville Chamberlain declares war on Nazi Germany/King George VI delivers a speech on the outbreak of World War II with the help of Lionel Logue at Buckingham Palace, London, England.

b) Schülervortrag

c) King George VI was a great King for he gained great popularity in World War II. As a conscientious and dedicated man he worked hard to adapt to his role as a King when he was suddenly thrown into it. This can be seen in the film when he outstandingly dedicates himself to Lionel's therapy in order to become a competent public speaker.
In contrast to his brother he was a very dutiful successor to the throne. George VI remained for most of the time at Buckingham Palace during World War II (despite the fact that it was bombed nine times) and so proved his loyalty to his people and hence set an example for them. Together with his wife he visited severely bombed areas in East London and in different places in the country. A close working relationship with Winston Churchill evolved when most of Europe fell to Hitler's Third Reich. When India and Pakistan became independent in 1947, George VI gave up his title as Emperor of India immediately.

Lösungsvorschlag zu *Copy 3* – *Elizabeth:*

chap.	when?	where?	what?	cinematic devices
1	31st October 1925	Wembley Stadium	supportive, accompanies him when he must deliver the speech; watches him the whole time	medium shots while Bertie is giving his speech
1	during the first doctor's treatment	in their living room	strong, as she speaks up to the doctor and asks questions; supportive, accompanies him during all therapies	establishing shot reading and watching the doctor and her husband, medium shot asking questions

chap.	when?	where?	what?	cinematic devices
2	unknown	Lionel's practice in Harley Street	caring, loving, helpful, finds Lionel for her husband; sophisticated: wears elegant clothes, jewellery; eloquent language	establishing shot coming into the practice, POV shot looking at Lionel; over-the-shoulder and reverse angle shots during their conversation
2	preparing for a party	at home	Bertie tells a bedtime story and Elizabeth makes sure that the daughters go to bed on time; strict, caring mother; shows herself to be a member of upper class with principles when talking about Wallis in the stairwell	medium shot, establishing shot listening to Bertie's story; tracking shot on the stairs
4	after Christmas Broadcast 1934	at home	Elizabeth comes in at night when Bertie is listening to the recording of his own voice made by Lionel Logue during his first session	zooming in on Elizabeth when Bertie's voice is heard as he stands in the door
4	after Christmas Broadcast 1934	Lionel's practice	Elizabeth and Bertie visit Lionel for a second time to negotiate the terms of his therapy "my husband has mechanical difficulties with his speech"	medium shot talking about therapy on the sofa
4		Lionel's practice	Bertie's therapy is shown and a speech he delivers at a factory is presented	cross-cutting; zooming in on Elizabeth sitting on Bertie; medium shots of Elizabeth sitting on Bertie and standing next to him on stage in the factory; full shots factory; medium shots shouting vowels out of the window and stopping the time
6		on the way to Balmoral	insecure, cares about what Wallis thinks about her and her weight	medium shot – in the car close-up – eating
6		Balmoral	traditional, old-fashioned, cannot accept Wallis as David's girlfriend; honest, tells Churchill what she thinks about Wallis without hesitating; remains true to herself, ignores Wallis	medium shot – coming in/saying hello to David medium shot of backs talking to Churchill, close-up talking about Wallis
8	11th December 1936	at home	listening to David's abdication speech on the radio	medium shot and zooming
8	after Bertie's first day	their house	Elizabeth prepares move to Buckingham Palace, attentive, asks him how his day was;	high-angle establishing shot – moving houses, medium/full shots – packing; close-up – talking to daughters, medium shot – Bertie comes in/over-the-shoulder shot; close-up – "How was it?" medium shot/close-up – listening to Bertie, panning

chap.	when?	where?	what?	cinematic devices
		study	encourages him when he doubts his qualities as a king; open and reserved, admits that she did not want to marry him at first because of his role and the attention that goes with it	
9	before coronation	at Lionel's flat	friendly, refined; casual and funny ("Ma'am as in ham"), as she talks to Myrtle informally and pours herself some tea	medium shot – standing in the door, full shot establishing shot – coming in, medium shot – having tea/talking to Myrtle
10	after coronation	Buckingham Palace private cinema	Elizabeth watches the film of Bertie's coronation with her family and Archbishop Lang	full shot, listening
11	3rd Sept. 1939	Buckingham Palace	supportive when Bertie delivers his speech	full shot – entering the room, medium shot – following Bertie, medium close-up – Bertie stammering, full shot – walking, medium shot – walking, full shot/medium shot/close-up – recording room, medium shot/full shot – listening, full shot/close-up – talking to Bertie, full shot – walking/ medium shot of the back / full shot of the back/ medium shot front-balcony

Lösungsvorschlag zu *Copy 3* – *Lionel:*

chap.	when?	where?	what?	cinematic devices
2	unknown	at his practice	casual when he first meets Elizabeth with regard to behaviour and language; looks: friendly; sure of himself as a speech therapist and determined ("my game, my turf, my rules"); likes to keep things simple: no receptionist	medium shots, reverse-angle shots/ over-the-shoulder shots, POV shots during the conversation with Elizabeth; establishing shots
2	unknown	at his flat with his family	loving, the way he cares for and talks to his children	medium shot during dinner, establishing shot of dining room
2	unknown	rehearsal	likes acting, but is not accepted in London despite being very good	establishing shot of the room, medium shot, medium close-up on Lionel on stage reciting Shakespeare

chap.	when?	where?	what?	cinematic devices
3	first session with Bertie	at his practice	unconventional, insists on calling Albert "Bertie" although Albert obviously does not approve; latest equipment, unorthodox, new methods; self-confident, insists on himself and Bertie being equals in his practice ("My castle, my turf, my rules"); funny, wants to bet with Bertie	establishing shot of therapy room, medium shot of Lionel when Bertie is sitting on the sofa, tracking shot while making tea, medium shots during recording; full shot after Bertie left
3		at his practice	negotiating the terms of his therapy; wants to see Bertie on a daily basis	low angle when speaking to Bertie and Elizabeth
4	next session with Bertie	at his practice at Harley Street	strict ("You have a short memory, Bertie!"); puts his cigarette out; peculiar: wants Bertie to sing	equal level; zooming in and out of different methods; medium shots shouting vowels out of a window
5	with his kids	in his practice	funny, when he re-enacts Shakespeare for his kids	close-up/medium shot playing Shakespeare/establishing shot
6	after King George V's death		good listener, when Bertie talks about his childhood; Australian son of a brewer; a good, honest friend, when he openly tells Bertie what he thinks about his future and that he should become King	medium shot – opening the door; low angle/close-up talking about Bertie's father, low angle sitting and talking about Bertie's childhood
7	after the party at Balmoral	in his practice	Bertie and Lionel talk about his problems with David	medium shot sitting on a chair, long shot – conversation, long shot/medium shot – when Bertie runs around swearing, tracking shot/ medium – when he decides to go out
7		in the park	while talking about Wallis Simpson Lionel suggests Bertie should become king; Bertie accuses him of treason and runs away leaving Lionel behind	establishing shot/long shot showing the two walking through the park; coming closer to the static camera, panning, medium shot of Lionel and Bertie talking about Wallis showing Lionel walking behind Bertie, handheld camera moves at the same time, medium shot of the backs and Lionel's hand touching Bertie – Lionel suggests Bertie should take the throne, camera movement stops, medium shot of the two, close-up – Bertie being angry/ close-up – Lionel explaining himself, medium shot, tracking shot

chap.	when?	where?	what?	cinematic devices
				– Bertie walking away and Lionel following him – first showing their backs, then their fronts when Bertie insults Lionel; Lionel does not walk anymore (long shot of him), medium shot looking sad, full shot of his back walking in the opposite direction
7		at home	talks to Myrtle about his problems with a patient	full shot sitting at a typewriter/establishing shot, medium close-up/close-up – talking to Myrtle
7		at Bertie's home	reflective: admits his mistakes and wants to apologize	medium shot – sitting and waiting, full shot /medium shot – talking to Bertie's servant
8		at his home	forgiving, forgives Bertie immediately; trustworthy and discreet, as he has never told Myrtle who his patient really is	establishing shot, full shot – preparing his home, medium shot – opening the door, establishing shot – presenting the parlour, medium shot – getting the shilling, talking to Bertie on equal level, medium close-up – talking about David and the Christmas broadcast, close-up – talking about fear, full shot – Myrtle arriving, medium shot – hiding behind door, medium shot – talking to Myrtle
9		Westminster Abbey	confident when he is doubted by Archbishop Lang; taught himself how to be a friend/listener by helping veterans after World War I, muscle therapy unorthodox/daring: sits on the throne in Westminster Abbey; encouraging and funny: practices coronation ceremony and makes Bertie laugh to release the pressure	establishing shot – meeting Archbishop Lang, medium shot – listening to and greeting Lang, walking towards and away from the static camera, medium shot of his legs – being accused of being a liar, medium shot/close-up – explaining himself, long shot – "lock me in the tower", long shot/medium shot – sitting on St. Edward's Chair, medium shot – standing up/talking to Lang/ medium close-up – Bertie's decision/"Thank you, Bertie", walking away from camera, bird's eye/ medium shot/long shot – going through speech, medium shot – dialogue between Bertie on the throne and Lionel far away, walking towards Bertie

chap.	when?	where?	what?	cinematic devices
10	3rd Sept 1939	Lionel's home	Lionel and his family listen to the declaration of war on the radio	establishing shot, static camera, Lionel walking back and forth, his hands touching Myrtle, medium shot, full shot zooming on his face – "is at war"
11	3rd Sept 1939	in the car	his son Laurie drives him to Buckingham Palace	medium shot – driving through London, POV – running people, handing out paper/medium shot
11	3rd Sept 1939	Buckingham Palace	supportive, practices the King's Speech with Bertie in a private room	tracking shot/high angle/long shot – coming in, walking away from the camera, medium shot – taking off his coat, medium shot/long shot/ establishing shot – walking and listening to Bertie, tracking shot – walking to Bertie and back, long shot – when Elizabeth comes in, long shot – when Bertie opens the door, medium shot when Bertie talks to Cosmo Lang, tracking shot/long shot – walking, long shot – when Bertie asks "how long?"
11	3rd Sept 1939	Buckingham Palace, during the speech	stays with him in the same room during the speech	establishing shot – room, medium shot – when he explains the microphone and talks to Bertie, close-up – "say it to me as a friend", medium shot – countdown, close-up from Bertie's POV – looking at Bertie nodding/giving him signals, medium shots – helping him, camera moving around the two, extreme close-up, close-up – smiling, medium shot zooming in – looking serous, medium shot – "very good", long shot – closing window, medium shot – "still stammer", POV through Lionel's eyes walking, long shot – when picture is taken, close-up – "friend", medium close-up – "thank you", medium close-up – when Elizabeth calls him Lionel, long shot – when Bertie walks to the other room, medium shot – nodding, close-up – looking at the balcony

Lösungsvorschlag zu *Copy 4* – *Bertie:*

chap.	when?	where?	what?	cinematic devices
1	during his first speech	Wembley Stadium	tense, helpless, stammering, trying to get the words out, speechless, insecure; dressed in black (suit, tie, coat, bowler)	high-angle shot when he approaches, point-of-view shot when he faces the microphone, close-ups, zooming on microphone (POV), over-the-shoulder shots while speaking
1	during the first therapy	in his house	smoking, skeptical, but willing to try, then furious ("bloody") and reluctant ("honestly, no more"); dressed in suit and tie	high-angle shots – smoking, speaking with marbles, tracking shot running away
2		at home	telling bedtime story to his daughters without greater impediments, relaxed, loving father (hugging his girls), later: flatly refusing any further treatment proposed by his wife	medium shot – coming in; establishing shot telling penguin story; medium close-ups telling the story
3		at Logue's practice	following his wife, looking around sceptically, admiring the planes Logue's sons made, sitting down not saying anything at first ("Waiting for me to commence a conversation one can wait rather a long wait."), tense, impatient, showing humour and self-mockery ("Timing isn't my stongest suit."), shocked at Lionel's lack of respect (Lionel wants to call him "Bertie" and wants them to be equal), easily frustrated, losing his temper, first not willing to cooperate, then more friendly and compliant ("You're not well acquainted with Royal Princes, are you?"), but finally giving up	establishing shot – showing the room; medium shots and full shots sitting on the sofa, high-angle shots on the sofa close-up to shoe scepticism; medium close-ups/close-ups reading; zooming in reading with music; close-up
3	Christmas Broadcast 1934	Sandringham	standing behind his father's desk, being shouted at by his father when trying to read ("Get it out, boy!"); foreshadowing of his future duties	full shot while father is reading; close-up to show he's sceptical and cannot read; medium shot reading; high angle when father talks to him
4		in his living room	desperate, then listening to his own voice on Logue's recording; pyjama and dressing gown, uncombed; Elizabeth, stunned, listening as well	zooming in on Bertie lying on the sofa; medium close-ups listening to his own recording

chap.	when?	where?	what?	cinematic devices
4		at Logue's practice, with Elizabeth on the sofa	("I'm willing to work hard, Doctor Logue… Are you willing to do your part?"), losing his temper, but still asking for assistance, cooper-ating and working hard	high angle; medium shots on the sofa
4		at Logue's practice	showing Lionel's therapy and a speech Bertie delivers at a factory	cross-cutting – therapy and a speech in a factory; camera on equal level; zooming in on different methods; zooming in a speech; zooming away from Elizabeth sitting on Bertie; medium shots on therapy/ close-up "mmmmmother"; close-up Bertie's shoes; full shots speech at the factory;
				medium shot on Bertie want-ing to take a break and smoke; medium shots shout-ing vowels out of a window; medium shot speech: close-up tongue-twisters; medium shot vowels; zooming in on Bertie's mouth saying "father"
5	1936	Sandring-ham	picks David up who arrives by plane; in the car with David towards Sandringham castle; in his father's room; having dinner with his mother and others; at his father's death bed, shocked and sad about his father's death	medium shot next to the plane; medium close-up in the car talking to David; medium shots at father's bed looking sad about his father's disease; medium shot smoking and at dinner; close-up crying about his father's death; establishing shot on the stairs with David; medium shot smoking
6	after his father's death	at Logue's practice	visiting Logue as someone he can trust, stammering, singing, continuing the construction of the plane as a reward, talking about his private life/childhood ("bloody agony"), sitting in a relaxed way, agreeing to call Logue 'Lionel' and no longer 'Doctor'	medium shot – coming in, medium close-up – asking for whiskey, low angle, close-up – talking about father, low angle – sitting together, high angle – painting plane
6		on the way to Balmoral	happy, relaxed, practicing tongue-twisters	medium shot – talking, close-up making a joke
6		Balmoral	at David's party, rather stiff, shocked about David's plan to marry Wallis, being mocked by David ("B-b-b-bertie")	medium shot – coming in; close-up – saying hello to Wallis, medium shot – saying hello to his brother, tracking shot – cellar, zooming close-up – getting to know about David's wedding plans; tracking shot, going upstairs, close-up "B-b-b-bertie"

chap.	when?	where?	what?	cinematic devices
7		in Lionel's practice	talking about David with Bertie	close-up high-angle – talking about David; long shot showing Lionel and Bertie, medium shot – swearing, tracking shot/medium/long shot – running around swearing
7		in the park	going for a walk with Logue, arguing because he does not want to hear that he could be King, calling it treason and insulting Lionel, smoking	long shot – Lionel and Bertie walking; Bertie is in front, static camera, the two walk towards the camera, medium shot – panning along the fountain, medium shot – tracking shot – talking about Wallis, Bertie in front, camera movement stops when Lionel touches Bertie, medium shot – Bertie's side – talking to Lionel angrily, zooming – close-up – treason, long shot – Bertie walking away fast (one sees his back), medium shot frontal – Bertie insults Lionel, medium close-up
7		at Bald-win's office	Prime Minister Baldwin tells Bertie that he and the government cannot accept the relationship between Wallis and Edward	long shot – getting out of the car, panning towards the door, establishing shot – 10 Downing Street, medium shot – listening and smoking, close-up – coughing, listening and asking questions
7		at his home	stammering when Churchill proposes he could be King and should call himself George VI after his father	establishing shot – in his study, close-up – with Churchill talking about war, David and his future name
7		Bucking-ham Palace	David tells him about his deci-sion to abdicate	long shot of David (Bertie is blurry in the front), medium shot – asking David a ques-tion, close-up – cannot accept it, not what he wanted, estab-lishing shot – David signing document (Bertie in the back), medium shot – walk-ing, establishing shot – sign-ing/medium shot, medium shot – standing in the room
8		at his home	listens to his brother's speech on the radio with his wife on the couch	medium shot, zooming in to close-up
8		on the way to the Accession Council	Bertie gets into the car and looks at photographers	medium shot frontal – walk-ing to the door, medium shot of Bertie's back – handheld camera, POV – reporter seeing Bertie getting into the car, zooming in on Bertie's face, POV – Bertie watching the people outside

chap.	when?	where?	what?	cinematic devices
8	12th Dec 1936	Accession Council	suffering under the burden of kingship, confronting the Council, lost, reading with a stammer; Royal Uniform	establishing shot – Bertie waiting, medium close-up/ long shot/medium shot/POV shot waiting, tracking shot following Bertie into the room, close-up – being nervous, high-angle shot – showing the many spectators, long shot – getting his text, close-up, POV shot – low angle – crowd, extreme close-up – starting his speech, POV – spectators/zooming to ancestors, extreme close-up
8	12th Dec 1936	his house	King George VI comes back home	establishing shot through the roof – Bertie comes back, medium shot – turning around the corner, POV – his daughters, close-up – talking to them, medium shot – kissing them, POV/medium shot – talking to Elizabeth
8	12th Dec 1936	at his desk	facing coronation, desperate ("I'm not a King. I'm a naval officer. It's the only thing I know about.")	close-up – sitting at his desk, different angles, medium shot, looking at paper with Elizabeth, zooming to close-up, different angles, extreme close-up focussing on Elizabeth and Bertie then and Elizabeth alternately
8		at Lionel's home	Bertie apologizes and wants to go on having therapy ("Waiting for a King to apologize, one can wait rather a long wait."), self-mocking ("Is the nation ready for two minutes of radio silence?"), extremely nervous ("bloody mess")	medium shot – Bertie and Elizabeth standing in front of Lionel's door, establishing shot – coming in, establishing shot – parlour, medium shot – Lionel and Bertie sitting in opposite chairs, medium shot – Bertie in his chair, medium close-up – talking from the side, medium close-up frontal, close-up – talking and listening, long shot – when Lionel hears Myrtle, long shot – Bertie standing up, medium shot – hiding behind the door, medium shot/medium close-up – when Elizabeth meets Myrtle, medium shot – sitting in chair, long shot – standing up and going through door, over-the-shoulder shot, Myrtle curtsying and Elizabeth talking, medium shot

chap.	when?	where?	what?	cinematic devices
9	before the coronation	Westminster Abbey	opposing the archbishop, doubting Logue's qualifications, then accepting Logue's explanation and rehearsing with him, relaxing	tracking shot/medium shot – Bertie's back, establishing shot – Archbishop greeting Bertie, POV (Lionel) watching Bertie's back, long shot – walking past camera, high-angle/medium shot, medium shot – introducing Logue, long shot – family box, medium close-ups, establishing shot – Lionel arriving, long shot – Bertie sitting on throne, medium shot, close-up, POV shot, close-ups, long shot – side – Lionel kneeling in front of Bertie, close-up, long shot – walking to camera, long shot (back) – walking away, close-up – doubts himself, panning towards Lionel, over-the-shoulder shot, long shot – walking, medium shot – his back, medium shot – accusing Lionel, close-up (frontal), medium shot (back), medium shot (frontal) – screaming, medium close-up, medium shot (back), POV, medium close-up, close-up – Archbishop Lang, medium shot (back) – listening, close-up – talking, over-the-shoulder shot, close-up, long shot – walking to the throne, establishing shot – sitting on the throne, long shot – listening to Lionel, long shot (from the side), medium shot, bird's-eye view – sitting on the throne, close-up, medium shot (side) focus on Lionel, medium shot of his front, long shot (frontal) – sitting on throne
10	after the coronation	at Buckingham Palace	watching newsreel; admiring Hitler's rhetoric power without understanding the content ("He seems to be saying it rather well.")	long shot – watching newsreel both focussing on the backs and focussing on the fronts from a high angle, medium close-up, long shots (frontal on equal level, backs from a high angle), medium close-ups – talking about Hitler
10	Baldwin resigns	at Buckingham palace	Bertie talks to PM Baldwin who regrets his appeasement policy and wants to resign	medium shot, medium close-up zooming in to close-up, close-up – when talking about his task

chap.	when?	where?	what?	cinematic devices
11	3rd Sept. 1939	at Buckingham Palace, in his office	Bertie gets his speech and wants Lionel to come	establishing shot – sitting at his desk, zooming in, POV – his speech, medium shot – wanting Logue to come, zooming in to close-up – reading silently
11	outbreak of World War II, 1939	Buckingham Palace, a private room	practising speech with Logue, desperate, but self-mocking ("I say that continuously, but no one listens."/"The solemnest King that's ever lived."), trying to relax by cursing, singing and waltzing	long shot – Bertie ready, establishing shot, medium shot – talking, handheld camera following Bertie, medium shot, medium shot, long shot – Lionel walking to Bertie, close-up – breathing and reading, long shot/close-up – swearing, medium shot – reading, long shot – singing, medium shot – swearing, zooming, medium shot/panning – waltzing, medium shot, long shot, long shot – Lionel and Bertie
11	3rd Sept 1939	Buckingham Palace, on his way to the recording room	Bertie walks to the recording room and meets many people including Churchill and Lang	zooming, medium shot – standing in the door, medium shot (back)/tracking shot – walking, medium shot/static camera – greeting Archbishop Lang, close-up – greeting Prime Minister Chamberlain, medium shot (back), close-up, medium shot (back), close-up, medium shot (frontal and back) – greeting Churchill, close-up, tracking shot/medium – walking with Churchill, medium shot/static camera – asking Lionel a question, long shot – walking through a room, POV – looking at hall, medium shot zooming in, tracking shot/close-up – frontal, tracking shot/medium – Bertie's back, close-up (frontal), medium shot (back), static camera/medium shot – greeting a man from the BBC, tracking shot
11	3rd Sept 1939	Buckingham Palace, recording room	Bertie delivers his speech with Lionel in the room	establishing shot, zooming in, close-up (side), extreme close-up through microphone, close-ups (side) – preparations, medium close-up (frontal), close-up (focus on Elizabeth),

chap.	when?	where?	what?	cinematic devices
				medium close-up (frontal), medium shot (side), close-up – kissing Elizabeth, close-up (front), POV – text, extreme close-ups, medium shot – thanking, medium shot – sighing, extreme close-ups – serious look, medium shot (side) – countdown, extreme close-ups – high angle, extreme close-up (without microphone in the picture), extreme close-up/panning (side), medium shot/zooming (side), panning, close-up with microphone angular, paning/ medium shot, zooming in, extreme close-ups (frontal), angular, zooming in, medium shot, zooming in/over the shoulder shot, angular close-up, extreme close-up (frontal) – sighing, medium shot (side) – getting coat, extreme close-ups (side) putting coat on/ making a joke
11	after the speech	Buckingham Palace	Bertie is relaxed, happy ("I inserted a few stammers so that they know it's me"), talks to people and shows himself with his family to his people on the balcony	medium shot/tracking shot – leaving the room, close-up/ tracking shot – taking congratulations, long shot – sitting down and taking picture, medium shot (side) – talking to Logue, medium close-up – thanking him, long shot – standing up, close-up – shaking hands, POV shot/ reverse-angle shot – talking, camera following him when Elizabeth comes in, close-up – kissing her, POV – when Elizabeth thanks Logue, tracking/ medium shot – talking to Churchill, Chamberlain and Lang, tracking shot/medium shot (back)/panning – kissing daughter Elizabeth,
				close-up, panning/close-up – kissing Margret, close-up, POV looking at Logue, medium shot (back)/tracking shot – going onto the balcony, medium shot (back) – on the balcony, long shot (back) – balcony, medium shot (front) – on the balcony, close-up – waving

Lösungsvorschlag zu *Copy 4* – *David:*

chap.	when?	where?	what?	cinematic devices
4	1934	Sandring-ham	father does not like David's seemingly happy relationship with Wallis	low angle of George V
5	1936	Sandring-ham	arrives by plane, pilot's dress (helmet, leather coat), busy, does not like his father to be ill as he does not want to become King; talks to Wallis on the phone, misses her, changes the clock to adjust the time (opposing his father's tradition), is approached by Cosmo Lang as the next King during dinner	medium shots/full shots arriving by plane; medium close-up – talking with his brother in the car and watching his sick father; medium shot phoning Wallis and changing the time; medium shots/medium close-ups – talking to Arch-bishop Lang during dinner
5	after George V's death	Sandring-ham	David is King, breaking down crying on his mother's shoulder, only thinking about his future with Wallis ("poor Wallis")	close-ups from a low angle when Davis realizes he is the King; medium shot crying on his mother's shoulder; medium shot saying "poor Wallis" on the stairs with Bertie
6		Balmoral	has a party with Wallis and other guests, leaves his brother as he has to serve Wallis, mocks Bertie ("B-b-b-bertie", "p-p-p-positively"), accuses him of wanting to push him from the throne	close-up – throwing a party, medium shot greeting first Elizabeth then Bertie, tracking shot – cellar, zooming/close-up – wedding plans, tracking shot – upstairs, close-up/over-the-shoulder shot B-b-b-ber-tie, medium/full shot – talking to Wallis
7	before abdication	Bucking-ham Palace	talks to Bertie about his decision, looks exhausted	full shot, panning, close-up – decision, panning
8	abdication 1936	Bucking-ham Palace	reads a radio broadcast, abdicates to live with the woman he loves	close-up/POV signing abdica-tion, medium shot smoking, panning – sitting in the broadcasting room, extreme close-up – reading
11	3rd Septem-ber 1939	(France) some-where at the sea	listening to Bertie's speech	establishing shot zooming in from afar to close-up – sitting on the sofa with Wallis

Lösungsvorschlag zu *Copy 5 – music:*

chap.	when? where? what?	music/sounds	atmosphere
1	in the stadium	quiet piano and violin during the speech, long notes as contrast to hard stammer	
2	in Logue's practice	piano and violin, slow, calm music	quiet atmosphere that started outside with the snow
2	Logue family in the dining room	fast, happy music (piano) that takes up successful treatment of George	positive, pleasant atmosphere in the family (Logue as a man you can trust)
3	Bertie and Lionel during treatment	fast classical music shows Bertie's progress, music is interrupted when speech is halting	
4	Bertie and Elizabeth at home	quiet, soft music introduces and prepares the way for the surprisingly good speech on the recording; quiet violin	relaxed calmness and relaxation
4	in Logue's practice/during the speech	faster and more complex music follows and underlines the progress of the treatment; music stops when stammer appears; finally music ends and treatment is successful: viewer identifies with Bertie's feelings during the treatment	positive, happy
4	Bertie and his family	slow rhythm, falling, represents death; high tunes show tears/mourning; deep ones show fear/despair	sad, desperate
5	Bertie and Lionel	long, calm bowed instruments during Bertie's report about his childhood (punishment); evoke pity, sadness	sad
6	Balmoral	happy piano music underlines party preparation, jazz to entertain the guests	carefree, happy and relaxed
7	Lionel and Bertie going for a walk	slow, calm music (piano, violin) as a contrast to Bertie's anger: development/Bertie's reaction comes as surprise to viewers	
7	Bertie and David	long tunes; calm violin music, first alone, then adding up, rising: underlines the development in the process;	very emotional

chap.	when? where? what?	music/sounds	atmosphere
8	during Bertie's speech	throughout the scene: long, calm bowed string instruments underline exclusively Bertie's perspective; Elizabeth's pity;	sad atmosphere evokes viewers' sympathy
8	Bertie and Elizabeth	slow music underlines, on the one hand, Bertie's despair and fear, on the other hand, Elizabeth's consolation, compassion, empathy	
8	at the Logues'	happy music accentuates the comfort imported by Lionel; he fills Bertie with courage; underlines unexpected, strange situation due to the huge differences between the families	
9	Bertie and Lionel in the Abbey	long, deep tunes combined with high piano notes	fear/excitement before coronation
10	Bertie and Lionel during the final rehearsal	fast, happy music as a precursor successful coronation	triumphant
10	Bertie and PM	calm, dark, mysterious music hints at war, his first conflict as King	serious, tense; rising tension
10	in the car	first calm music during the radio announcement, parallel to Hitler's voice the tension rises; sirens	apprehension, anxiety
10	Bertie and Lionel during the speech	long, deep notes at the beginning fill the gaps in Bertie's speech (when he hesitates); music accompanies structure of the speech; the grave occasion and Lionel's composure are underlined; slowly rising melody (bowed instruments) expresses pride in the nation/the people's pride in their country (reflected in Bertie's words)	overall sadness and disappointment because of war
11	Bertie and entourage on the way to the balcony	serene music, accentuated by single notes shows Bertie's success/victory over stammer; faster piano music at the end	hopeful future of England

Who says what? – viewing activity

Match the speech bubble with the correct character.

Bertie – Lionel – Myrtle – Winston Churchill – David – Elizabeth – Wallis – King George V – Prime Minister Baldwin – Archbishop Lang – Queen Mary

You needn't be governed by fear.

And we need a king who we can all stand behind united.

Perhaps he doesn't want to be a great.

Your services are no longer required.

It was a relief knowing I wouldn't be King.

I have found it impossible to carry the heavy burden of responsibility

None of this unpleasantness would be tolerated.

And the King, as Head of the Church of England, cannot marry a divorced woman.

We've become actors.

She calls me the fat Scottish cook.

Oh, how lovely to see you both.

Long-term viewing-task: Historical events

Timeline listing important historical events in Bertie's life

a) List the most important historical events that are mentioned in the film (e.g. 1925: British Empire Exhibition).

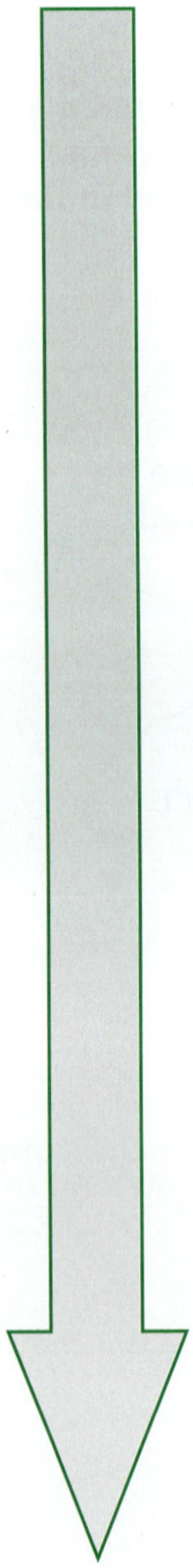

b) Be prepared to give a short presentation in class about these topics.

c) "If the 'greatness' of a King can be measured by the extent to which his qualities correspond to the needs of a nation at a given moment in history, then George VI was a great King, and perhaps a very great King."

Explain this statement written by René Massigli, Ambassador of France to the Court of St. James's, two weeks after the King's death.

Long-term viewing-tasks: Characterization of …

Describe how ____ is presented in the film. Pay special attention to his/her behaviour, choice of words, and opinions as well as his/her outward appearance. In what way does he/she develop in the film?
Fill in the grid below while watching the film in your English sessions. Note down differences after each session.

when?	where?	what?	cinematic devices

Long-term viewing-tasks: Development

Describe how ______________________________ is presented in the film. Pay special attention to his/her development. Make notes on his/her behaviour, choice of words, and opinions as well as his/her outward appearance at the beginning of the film as opposed to the end of the film. When do you realize changes and how does the character change? Fill in the grid below while watching the film in your English sessions. Note down differences after each session.

when?	where?	what?	cinematic devices

Long-term viewing-task: Filmmusic and sounds

Take notes on the music and sounds used in the film. Which atmosphere is created with the help of sounds and types of music in different scenes.
Make notes on the type of music (e. g. instrumental/classical…) and the kind of instruments that are used. Characterize the music (e. g. complex, monotonous, repetitive, etc.). Note down special sounds and their effects, too. Can you recognize a musical motif that is used in different scenes?

when? where? what?	music/sounds	atmosphere

The language of film: Selected terms for film analysis

1 Camera/image

1.1 Field sizes (*Einstellungsgröße/Bildausschnitt*)

extreme long shot *(Weitaufnahme/Panoramaaufnahme)*: a view from a considerable distance, eg. the skyline of a city

long shot *(Totale)*: the camera is at a great distance from the subject being filmed and presents the entire setting

full shot *(Halbtotale):* a full view of a person; includes the entire body of a subject and not much else

American shot *(Amerikanische):* a three-quarter view of a person, showing her or him from the knees up

medium shot *(Nahaufnahme):* a view of the upper half of a person's body

close-up *(Großaufnahme)*: the camera is very close to the object; full view of, typically, a human face

extreme close-up/detail shot *(Detailaufnahme)*: a small object or part of an object shown large (a speaking mouth, a telephone number on an envelope)

1.2 Point of view (*Darstellungsperspektive*) establishing shot

generally a long shot that shows the general location of the scene that follows, often providing essential information, and orienting the viewer

point-of-view shot (POV): shows the scene from the point of view of a character

over-the-shoulder shot: the camera gets close to, but not fully into, the viewing position of a character

reaction shot: a shot showing a character reacting (with wonder, amusement, annoyance, horror, etc.) to what she/he has just seen

reverse-angle shot: a shot from the opposite side of a subject

1.3 Camera angles (*Kameraperspektive*)

eye-level/straight-on angle (*Normalsicht/Augenhöhe*): the camera is positioned at about the same height as the object (fairly conventional)

high angle/overhead *(Obersicht/Vogelperspektive)*: objects and people are filmed from above; a limit case is a bird's-eye view taken from a helicopter or an airplane

low angle/below shot (*Untersicht/Froschperspektive*): objects and people are filmed from below

1.4 Camera movement (*Kamerabewegung*)

pan(ning) (*horizontaler Schwenk*): the camera moves from left to right or vice versa around the vertical axis

tilt (*vertikaler Schwenk*): the camera moves upwards (tilt up) or downwards (tilt down) around the horizontal axis

tracking shot/pulling shot (*Kamerafahrt*): the camera follows (tracks) or precedes (pulls) an object which is in motion itself

push in, pull back: the camera moves in on or away from a stationary object

zoom: not a camera movement, but a shift in the focal length of the camera lens to give the impression that the camera is getting closer to (zooming in) or farther from (zooming out) an object

1.5 Camera speed (Aufnahmegeschwindigkeit)

normal speed (*normale Geschwindigkeit*): the speed of the action corresponds to its real time **slow motion** (*Zeitlupe*): the action takes more time than in reality; it is slowed down

fast motion (*Zeitraffer*): the action takes less time than in reality

freeze frame (*Standbild*): a still picture

1.6 Colour (Farbgestaltung)

black and white (*schwarz-weiß*)

colour (*Farbe*)

predominance of certain shades and tones (*Einfärbung*)

1.7 Lighting (Beleuchtung, Lichtgestaltung)

high key vs. low key (*starke vs. geringe Grundausleuchtung*): the whole scene is fully lit vs. not everything is fully lit (= indirect lighting, a certain darkness of the screen)

natural vs. studio light (*Tageslicht vs. Kunstlicht*)

2 Montage/editing

shot (*Einstellung*): the basic unit of a film; an uninterrupted sequence of action shown continuously
sequence (*Sequenz*): a larger unit of film composed of a number of shots which belong together (because of time, actors involved, setting, etc.)
cut (*Schnitt*): most common type of transition in which one scene ends and a new one immediately begins; a cut is the pump from one shot to the next
fade out (*Abblendung*)… **fade in** (*Aufblendung*): the end of a shot is marked by fading out to an empty screen (usually black); there is a brief pause; then a fade in introduces the next shot
dissolve (*Überblendung*): a gradual transition in which the end of one scene is superimposed over the beginning of a new one
parallel action/cross-cutting (*Parallelmontage*): intermingling the shots of two or more scenes **flashback** (*Rückblende*): a sequence of a film that goes back in time to show what happened earlier in the story
flash-forward (*Vorausschau*): scenes or shots referring to future time
match cut: two shots or scenes are linked by visual, aural or metaphorical parallelism

Nünning, A./Surkamp, C.: Englische Literatur unterrichten – Grundlagen und Methoden, Friedrich Verlag GmbH, Seelze 2006

Field sizes

extreme long shot
↓
long shot
↓
full shot
↓
medium shot
↓
close-up

Camera movement

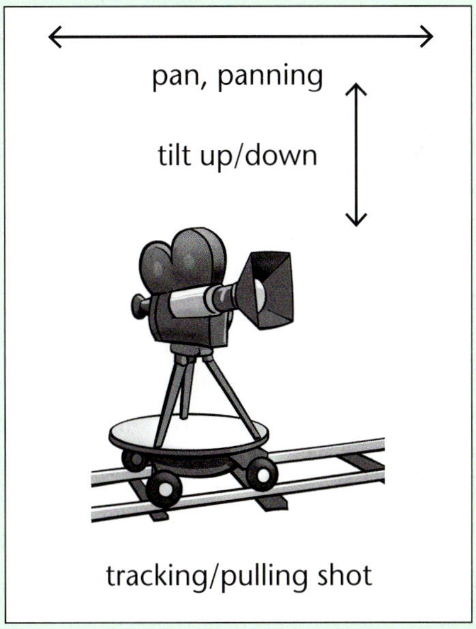

Camera angles

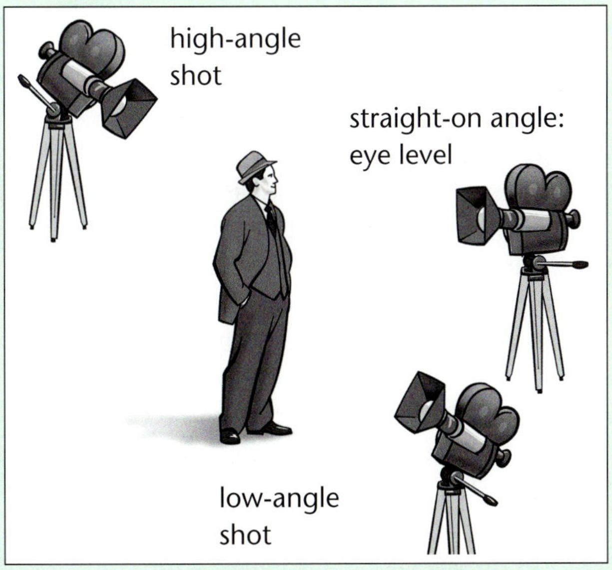

Component 2

Introducing a prince's life

Dieses *Component* soll den Schülerinnen und Schülern die Welt des englischen Königshauses, die im Film präsentiert wird, näher bringen und wesentliches Hintergrundwissen über das politische System in Großbritannien und über die Rolle des Monarchen vermitteln, sodass Teile des in Nordrhein-Westfalen obligatorischen Abiturthemas „Britain's past and present: from Empire to Commonwealth, monarchy and modern democracy" mit dieser Einheit abgedeckt werden können.

2.1 The political system of the United Kingdom

Dieser Teil verschafft einen Überblick über die politischen Parteien im Vereinigten Königreich und thematisiert die Gewaltenteilung ebenso wie das Grundverständnis von Demokratie und das Wahlsystem.
In einem ersten Schritt könnte daher gemeinsam mit den Schülerinnen und Schülern über ihr Demokratieverständnis diskutiert werden. Zu Beginn kann beispielsweise das Wort *democracy* als stummer Impuls an der Tafel präsentiert werden. Neben der Herleitung aus dem Griechischen (*the rule of the people*), die eventuell von der Lehrperson ergänzt werden muss, können bereits hier wesentliche Merkmale wie *elections, freedom of opinion and expression, guarantee of basic human rights like equality before the law or absence of slavery and torture* gesammelt werden.
Ausgehend von dem Schaubild (***Copy 7***) wird anschließend die konkrete Umsetzung eines demokratischen Systems im United Kingdom beschrieben.

Lösungsvorschlag zu *Copy 7*:

The United Kingdom has a constitutional monarchy, in which the Queen or King is the head of state and the Prime Minister the head of government. The power is separated into four branches, the monarch, the parliament, the government and the judiciary/supreme court. The monarch appoints the Prime Minister, the members of the supreme court and the aristocrats that form the House of Lords. Furthermore, the monarch can formally dissolve the government, on the advice of the Prime Minister. The cabinet is formed by about 20 ministers and the leader of the strongest party, the Prime Minister (who appoints his cabinet himself). The Cabinet puts forward laws and essentially runs the government. Every five years all citizens over the age of 18 can vote, hence the members of Parliament (MPs) are elected in a first-past-the-post system. The House of Commons creates the laws and is able to elect the Prime Minister. The Prime Minister can dissolve the parliament. The House of Commons and the House of Lords together form the parliament. The task of the House of Lords is to approve the laws made by the House of Commons. The House of Lords has 700 members consisting of life peers, bishops, hereditary peers etc.

Als Erweiterung kann anschließend ein Vergleich zum deutschen System hergestellt werden, um den Schülerinnen und Schülern die Unterschiede bzw. Gemeinsamkeiten zu verdeutlichen. Je nach Kenntnisstand der Lerngruppe bieten sich hier eventuell Kurzreferate zu dieser Fragestellung oder eine Ausarbeitung in der Hausaufgabe an.

Compare the political systems of Germany and of the United Kingdom.

Möglicher Tafelanschrieb/Lösungsvorschlag:

similarities	differences
general elections (every four or five years)	British head of state is the monarch, German head of state is elected
first chambers (House of Commons and Bundestag) elect the head of government and make laws	second chambers: House of Lords which can suggest changes to the laws and is not elected vs Bundesrat which has more legislative power
	UK: majority system, Germany: majority and proportional system

2.2 Duties of the monarch

Im folgenden Schritt werden die Aufgaben und Pflichten des *British Sovereign* herausgearbeitet, um den Schülern weitere Facetten der Aufgabenbereiche zu veranschaulichen. Bei der späteren Besprechung der Szenen, in denen Bertie mit diversen dieser Anforderungen ringt, kann hierauf Bezug genommen werden. Zur Veranschaulichung kann, falls gewünscht, bereits vor Einstieg in den Film die Szene von Alberts erstem Auftritt als König in Kombination mit dem Text (***Copy 8***) dienen, die in der gewählten Aufgabenform an das Klausurenformat angepasst ist, sodass die Schülerinnen und Schüler die entsprechenden Aufgabenstellungen bereits üben können *(tasks no. 1 & 2a)*. Falls die Lerngruppe jedoch wenig Vorwissen und Vorerfahrung zur Filmanalyse mitbringt, kann der vorliegende Text ebenfalls als Grundlage einer vertiefenden Hausaufgabe dienen, da die Aufgaben und Pflichten des *British Sovereign* detailliert dargelegt werden *(tasks no. 1 & 2b)* und nur der *screenshot*, der aus der o. a. Szene entnommen ist und an dieser Stelle als Bild analysiert wird (German DVD 1:10:25; English DVD 1:09:37), den auf Georg VI lastenden Druck bereits eindrucksvoll verdeutlicht.

1:09:09 – 1:14:13
German DVD

1:08:29 – 1:10:07
English DVD

Lösungsvorschlag zu *Copy 8*:

1. Head of State: "constitutional and representational duties": duties within the country: opening of Parliament; approval of Orders in Council; signing Acts of Parliament; meetings with the Prime Minister – duties worldwide: representing Great Britain; receiving ambassadors; entertaining visiting Heads of State; visiting other countries (Head of Commonwealth)
   Head of Nation: focus for national identity, providing stability and continuity; distinguishing and honouring achievements; visiting parts of the United Kingdom; representing the people (Supreme Gouvernor of the Church of England)
2. a) In the given screenshot the duties are portrayed as overwhelming as the scene is filmed from a high angle. George VI is standing opposite many other men and he has just one person at his side, which shows how lonely

the position of a king is. Furthermore, the whole picture is very gloomy and dark apart from the golden ceiling which represents the long family history and creates an intimidating atmosphere. All his ancestors are watching George VI when he has to fulfil his first duty as a king.

b) The toll on Bertie seems to be heavy as his facial expressions seem very tense on his way to the car. Both the people on the streets and the people making up the Accession Council at St James's Palace expect a great deal of him and do not look friendly. Bertie is presented in a high-angle shot which stresses the pressure he is feeling. The spectators are presented in low-angle shots so that they seem larger than Bertie. Both the enormous crowd and the zooming ins on the portraits of his ancestors (e.g. Queen Victoria and his father George V) seem to intimidate Bertie. The duty of being a King has many consequences, Bertie and his family must move to Buckingham Palace and his children Margaret and Elizabeth must treat him differently now (e.g. the girls must curtsy). In the evening he can open up to his wife Elizabeth and his duties seem to be overwhelming: the Christmas broadcast, the coronation, finances and politics. Bertie realizes that he is just a naval officer and has not been prepared for his role as King. The hopelessness of the situation is underlined by zooming in on the couple and full shots of both their faces.

Im Anschluss sollen die Schülerinnen und Schüler sich exemplarisch mit wegweisenden Entscheidungen der drei Könige George V, Edward VIII und George VI beschäftigen und diese vor dem historischen Hintergrund einordnen bzw. persönlich bewerten. Nachdem in den letzten Schritten deutlich wurde, dass dieses Amt, in das man sich wohlgemerkt nicht wählen lassen kann, sondern das man erbt, diverse Arbeitsbereiche umfasst, werden hier Interdependenzen zwischen den Aufgaben und Pflichten, den persönlichen Entscheidungen und den Auswirkungen auf das Volk deutlich. Die Schülerinnen und Schüler können die Loyalität der Könige hinsichtlich der ihnen übertragenen Aufgaben und Rollen betrachten und bereits Aspekte aus späteren Teilen des Films spekulativ aufgreifen, wie z. B. die Frage, ob Edward VIII zurücktreten wollte, weil er das Amt des Königs als zu einengend und belastend empfand oder diesen Schritt eher aufgrund von äußeren Zwängen getan hat.
Die notwendigen Hintergründe zum Leben der drei Könige können entweder in einer Erarbeitungsphase im Internet recherchiert werden oder der Lerngruppe als Materialgrundlage (***Copy 9***) zur Verfügung gestellt werden. Ein arbeitsteiliges Vorgehen, bei dem sich die Schülerinnen und Schüler jeweils nur einem Monarchen widmen, ermöglicht eine anschließende Präsentationsphase in Dreiergruppen. Auch die Diskussion der Einflüsse bzw. Auswirkungen kann in diesen Kleingruppen stattfinden.

Decisions made by each of the three kings – George V, Edward VIII and George VI – had influences on their own and many other people's lives: George V changed the family name, Edward VIII abdicated, and George VI sought the help of a speech therapist.
Discuss in how far their respective positions affected their decisions? To what extent were they influenced by society? And what message did their decision send to the nation?

Die relativ offene Fragestellung lässt verschiedene Ansätze zu. Die Entscheidung von George V muss einerseits sicherlich als Ausdruck seiner ablehnenden Haltung der deutschen politischen Entwicklungen gegenüber gesehen werden, kann aber andererseits auch eine Botschaft an seine englischen Untertanen sein, in der er die Briten quasi als seine Familie annimmt. Etwas zwiespältiger ist eventuell die Einstellung der Schülerinnen und Schüler zu Edward VIII, der sich einerseits gar nicht von seinem Amt hat beeinflussen lassen und seinen

Gefühlen den Vorrang gegeben hat, der aber andererseits natürlich ohne diese Position nicht in eine solche Zwangslage geraten wäre. Seine relativ schnelle Abdankung kann auch als Flucht aus einem ohnehin ungeliebten Amt gesehen werden. Unter Einbeziehung der in der Kopiervorlage angeführten Zitate wird besonders deutlich, wie viel pflichtbewusster George VI seine Rolle sieht, auf die er, im Gegensatz zu seinem älteren Bruder, eigentlich gar nicht vorbereitet war. Seine ganz persönliche Entwicklung wurde gewiss durch die Übernahme der Rolle als König beeinflusst, aber im Gegenzug stellte er sein (eigentlich) privates Streben nach Verbesserung auch öffentlich dar.

2.3 The Windsors

In diesem Teil geht es um eine Ausweitung der Beschäftigung mit der königlichen Familie auf die heutige Zeit. Den Schülerinnen und Schülern soll bewusst werden, dass einzelne im Film dargestellte Personen – z. B. Queen Elizabeth II – heute noch leben. Zur Verdeutlichung kann ***Copy 10*** dienen, die den Stammbaum der Familie Windsor von George V bis heute zeigt.
Um den Bezug zu den in vielen Medien präsenten und damit häufig vertrauten Personen herzustellen, wird mit einer (Internet-)Recherche begonnen, in der die besondere Stellung in der Gesellschaft, die Betätigungsfelder und Aufgaben der einzelnen Mitglieder der *Royal Family* herausgearbeitet werden (***Copy 11***). Mögliche Internetquellen sind z. B.:

- http://www.royal.gov.uk/ThecurrentRoyalFamily/Overview.aspx
- http://www.princeofwales.gov.uk/
- http://en.wikipedia.org/wiki/British_Royal_Family
- http://www.britroyals.com/

Hier sollten sich die Schülerinnen und Schüler wieder arbeitsteilig über die verschiedenen Personen informieren. Falls eine Recherchearbeit nicht möglich ist, besteht auch die Möglichkeit, den Erwartungshorizont als Kopie auszuteilen (***Copy 12***).
In der sich der Arbeitsphase anschließenden Präsentationsphase sollen die Schülerinnen und Schüler ihre Ergebnisse adressaten- und sachgerecht vorstellen, wobei die Einübung und Weiterentwicklung von *presentation skills* zum Tragen kommt. Falls die Zeit im Unterricht nicht ausreicht, kann die Erarbeitung selbstverständlich auch in die Hausaufgabe verlagert werden.
Analog zu der Behandlung der heutigen Königsfamilie sollten die Schülerinnen und Schüler auch Hintergrundwissen über die historischen Personen des Films erwerben, sodass die folgenden Informationen entweder ebenfalls recherchiert oder auch dem Kurs in anderer Form zur Verfügung gestellt werden. Denkbar sind hier zum Beispiel Lückentexte (in denen einzelne Informationen oder die Namen der Personen fehlen, ***Copy 13***) oder ein Gruppenpuzzle, für das die Lerngruppe in Kleingruppen aufgeteilt wird, in denen jeder Schüler sich das Wissen zu einer Person aneignet und dieses anschließend seinen Mitschülern präsentiert.

2.4 Bertie: The Prince's Speech

Im nächsten Schritt soll die erste Szene des Films analysiert werden, in der die Hintergründe zu den Aufgaben eines Königs verdeutlicht werden (***Copy 14***). Der junge Albert muss in der Funktion des *Duke of York* eine Rede zur Eröffnung der *Empire Exhibition* halten. Diese royale Pflicht fällt ihm sichtlich schwer, da er seit seiner Kindheit an einem Sprachfehler leidet. Durch diese erste Filmszene gelingt es den Schülern trotz der Distanz zum Königshaus, sich in Albert hineinzuversetzen, da dieser durch sein Stottern sehr menschlich wirkt. Der Filmausschnitt ist darüber hinaus auch filmtechnisch sehr reizvoll, da der Zuschauer eher den

Eindruck erhält, Albert befinde sich auf dem Weg zu seiner Hinrichtung als zu einem öffentlichen Auftritt im Radio. Falls die Schüler eine Auffrischung filmanalytischer Begriffe benötigen, bietet sich ***Copy 6*** als Hilfe oder vorbereitende Hausaufgabe an.

German DVD 0:00:56–0:05:20

English DVD 0:00:30–0:04:52

Die Schüler sollten die erste Filmszene zweimal präsentiert bekommen. Während des ersten Betrachtens sollten sie sich Notizen zu der Handlung und den besonderen Geräuschen sowohl vor der Rede als auch während der Rede machen. Bei der zweiten Betrachtung der Szene sollte der Fokus auf den Kameraeinstellungen liegen. Schnelle Schüler können sich im Rahmen der Binnendifferenzierung bereits mit den Aufgaben 2 und 3 auf ***Copy 14*** befassen. In starken Kursen schließt sich nun die Besprechung der Ergebnisse an. In schwächeren Kursen kann eine kurze Partnerarbeitsphase zwischengeschaltet werden, in der sich die Schüler über ihre Ergebnisse austauschen.

Lösungsvorschlag zu *Copy 14:*

ad 1.	1st viewing		2nd viewing
	action	**sound**	**camera**
before the speech • BBC news reader	prepares himself, gargles, spits; practises talking, introduces Bertie flawlessly	piano atomizer silence introduction	different angles, establishing shot close-ups, long shot
• Bertie	leans against the wall with Elizabeth, learns his text, practises, kisses his wife, climbs the stairs, looks at microphone	is called Archbishop supports him piano slows down silence	high angle → makes Bertie seem smaller close-ups → to show his feelings
during the speech	Bertie looks at light and tries to deliver his speech Elizabeth looks at him desperately people in the crowd watch him expectantly and later seem to be ashamed Archbishop desperate	silence horse neighs dramatic music violins stammering	POV shot long shot → people close-ups pan through crowd establishing shot → soldiers

2. tense, excited, expectant, disappointed, nervous, attentive atmosphere; created by handheld camera, close-ups; high-angle shots

3. introducing the main character, his role and his problem: a speech impediment

Um die Unterschiede zwischen den beiden parallelen Welten der *Royals* und der Untertanen deutlicher herauszustellen, werden im nächsten Schritt die Lebensumstände von Bertie und Elizabeth und von Lionel Logue und seiner Familie anhand von ausgewählten Szenen (Logue und Albert in ihrer Rolle als Familienväter) verglichen, sodass der unterschiedliche Hintergrund der beiden Charaktere herausgearbeitet wird. Dies ist besonders wichtig, da sich zum einen eine ungewöhnliche Freundschaft entwickelt und zum anderen den Schülern ein Einblick in die Lebensumstände einer königlichen Familie und einer gewöhnlichen Familie in den 30er-Jahren in England gewährt wird. Dazu bietet sich eine arbeitsteilige Gruppenarbeit an. Zunächst betrachten die Schüler die gleiche Szene mit verschiedenen Aufgabenstellungen (***Copy 15 a*** und ***b***). Im Anschluss stellen sie sich gegenseitig ihre Ergebnisse vor und vergleichen das Leben der Royals mit dem der gewöhnlichen Briten.

German DVD
12:04–15:58

English DVD
11:52–14:59

Compare the life of a Royal Highness with that of a commoner.

Lösungsvorschläge zu *Copies 15 a* und *15 b*:

Beim Zusammentragen der Ergebnisse kann folgender Tafelanschrieb entstehen:

1.

	royals	**commoners**
personnel	Bertie and Elizabeth have many servants (e.g. maid, governess, driver)	Lionel does not even have a secretary
housing	they live in a big house/palace with nice furniture and wallpaper underlined by good lighting and a fire to create a warm atmosphere	they live in a small flat; Lionel's practice is very simple underlined by gloomy dark colours
language	Elizabeth uses sophisticated/ elevated English	Lionel uses colloquial words like "loo" and "hubby"
clothing	Bertie and Elizabeth wear very stylish, expensive clothes (e.g. fur coat)	Lionel wears normal, rather simple clothes
duties	Bertie and Elizabeth must attend parties and formal meetings	Lionel must work as a speech therapist when what he loves most is being an actor
children	Elizabeth and Margaret have many toys	Lionel's children have to help in the household

➡ There are many differences between lower- and upper-class life but both love their children dearly.

2. function of the scenes: showing the difference between Bertie and Lionel

The Political System of the United Kingdom

The **United Kingdom** (of Great Britain and Northern Ireland) is a **constitutional monarchy** in which the **monarch is the head of state** and **the Prime Minister is the head of government**. The UK has been a multi-party system since the 1920s, the two largest parties being the Conservative Party and the Labour Party.

Political parties

The Conservative Party	Labour Party
• centre-right • conservatism • British Unionism (against Scottish and Welsh independence) • opposition to the Euro, strong defense of Pound Sterling • Eurosceptic position • free-market policy • criticism of Labour's state multiculturalism	• left to centre-left • democratic socialist party • supports government intervention in the economy • for redistribution of wealth • advocates increased rights for workers • favours an extended welfare state • support of multiculturalism

The U.K. system of government (separation of powers)

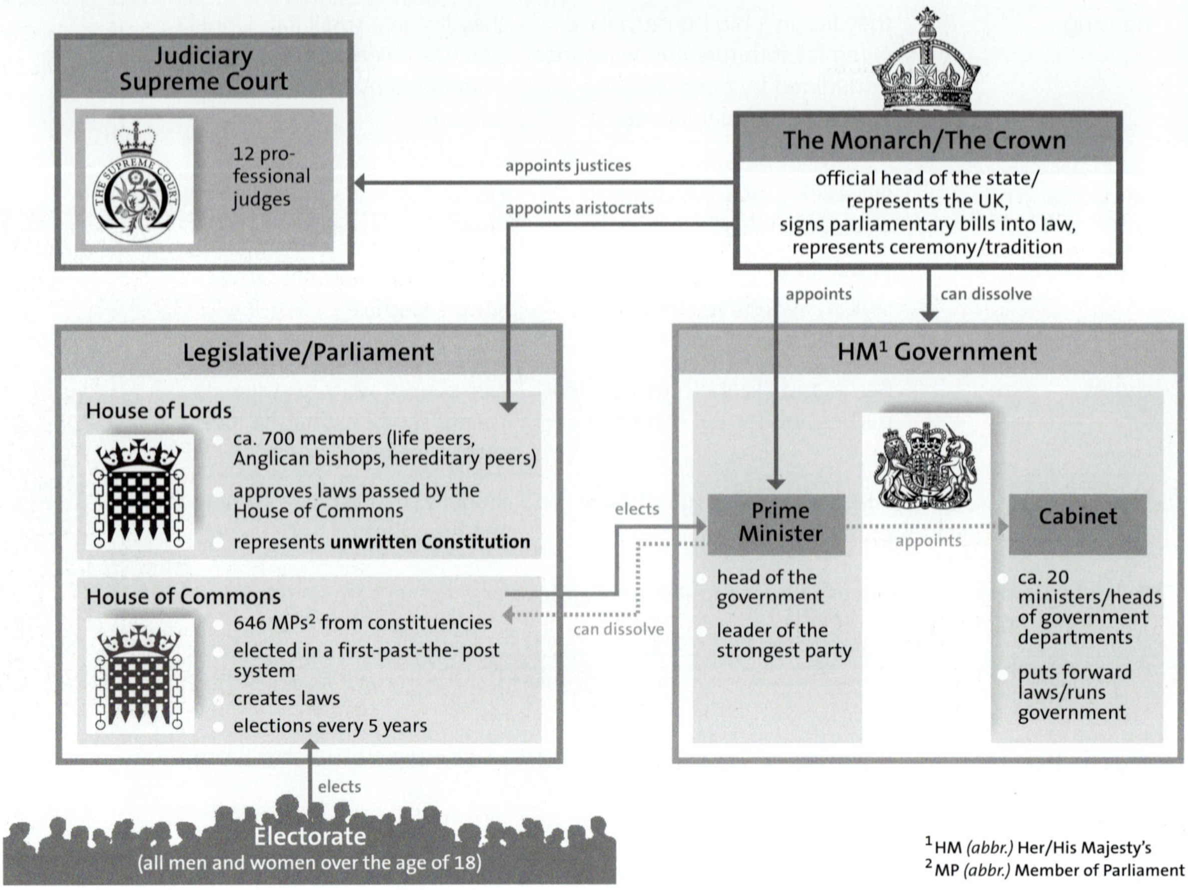

[1] HM *(abbr.)* Her/His Majesty's
[2] MP *(abbr.)* Member of Parliament

With a partner, describe the political system of Great Britain.

The Role of the British Sovereign

The British Sovereign can be seen as having two roles: Head of State, and 'Head of the Nation'. As Head of State, The Queen undertakes constitutional and representational duties which have developed over one thousand years of history.
There are inward duties, with The Queen playing a part in State functions in Britain. Parliament must be opened, Orders in Council have to be approved, Acts of Parliament must be signed, and meetings with the Prime Minister must be held.
There are also outward duties of State, when The Queen represents Britain to the rest of the world. For example, The Queen receives foreign ambassadors and high commissioners, entertains visiting Heads of State, and makes State visits overseas to other countries, in support of diplomatic and economic relations. (…)
As 'Head of Nation', The Queen's role is less formal, but no less important for the social and cultural functions it fulfils. These include: providing a focus for national identity, unity and pride; giving a sense of stability and continuity; recognising success, achievement and excellence; and supporting service to others, particularly through public service and the voluntary sector. These roles are performed through different types of engagement. By means of regular visits through every part of the United Kingdom, The Queen is able to act as a focus for national unity and identity.
Through her engagements and walkabouts, The Queen is able to meet people from every walk of life. The Queen's unifying role as Sovereign is also shown in her special relationships with the devolved assemblies in Scotland and Wales.
In addition, at times of national celebration or tragedy, The Queen publicly represents the nation's mood – for example, at the annual commemoration of the war dead on Remembrance Sunday, or at celebrations for a national sporting victory.
The Queen also has an essential role in providing a sense of stability and continuity in times of political and social change. The system of constitutional monarchy bridges the discontinuity of party politics. While political parties change constantly, the Sovereign continues as Head of State, providing a stable framework within which a government can introduce wide-ranging reforms.
With more than five decades of reading State papers, meeting Heads of State and ambassadors and holding a weekly audience with the Prime Minister, The Queen has an unequalled store of experience upon which successive Prime Ministers have been able to draw. The Queen is able to recognise success and achievement in a personal way. These include honours, awards, visits, patronage and sponsorship. At Investitures, for example, The Queen honours individuals for public service or outstanding achievement. […]
The Queen also supports service to others, through close relationships with the voluntary and charitable sector. About 3,000 organisations list a member of the Royal Family as patron or president. The Queen has over 600 patronages and The Duke of Edinburgh over 700.
In all these roles, The Queen is supported by members of the Royal Family, who carry out many of the engagements which The Queen cannot undertake in person.

Source: http://www.royal.gov.uk/monarchuk/howthemonarchyworks/theroleofthesovereign.aspx [04 12 2012]

1. Sum up the role of the British Sovereign.
2. a) Analyse how the duties are portrayed in the given screenshot.
   b) Analyse how the duties are portrayed in the given film scene.

The Royal Family: Biographical information

George V

Title: King of the United Kingdom and the British Dominions; Emperor of India

Full Name: George Frederick Ernest Albert; in 1917 during World War I anti-German sentiment led King George V to change the family name from the Germanic Saxe-Coburg-Gotha to Windsor.

Born: June 3, 1865 at Marlborough House, London

Parents: Edward VII and Alexandra of Denmark

Relation to Elizabeth II: grandfather

Ascended to the throne: May 6, 1910; crowned: June 22, 1911 at Westminster Abbey

Married: Mary, the daughter of the Duke of Teck

Children: five sons including Edward VIII and George VI, and one daughter

Died: January 20, 1936 at Sandringham, Norfolk, aged 70 years

Quotes: 'After I am dead, the boy will ruin himself in twelve months' – about his son Edward who became Edward VIII; 'Try living on their wages before you judge them' – taking exception to the suggestion that workers involved in the General Strike were revolutionaries; 'I cannot understand it, after all I am only a very ordinary sort of fellow' – on adulation from cheering crowds on the occasion of his Silver Jubilee

Edward VIII

Title: King of the United Kingdom and the Dominions of the British Commonwealth; Emperor of India

Full Name: Edward Albert Christian George Andrew Patrick David

Born: June 23, 1894 at White Lodge, Richmond, Surrey

Parents: George V and Mary of Teck

Relation to Elizabeth II: uncle

Ascended to the throne: Jan 20, 1936, aged 41 years; uncrowned

Abdicated: Dec 11, 1936

Married: Ms Wallis Simpson

Died: May 28, 1972 at Paris, aged 77 years

Quotes: 'I wanted to be an up-to-date king. But I didn't have much time.'; 'I have found it impossible to carry the heavy burden of responsibility and to discharge my duties as king as I would wish to do without the help of the woman I love.' – abdication speech; 'Of course, I do have a slight advantage over the rest of you. It helps in a pinch to be able to remind your bride that you gave up a throne for her.'

George VI

Title: King of the United Kingdom and the Dominions of the British Commonwealth; Emperor of India; Head of the Commonwealth

Full Name: Albert Frederick Arthur George

Born: December 14, 1895 at Sandringham, Norfolk

Parents: George V and Mary of Teck

Relation to Elizabeth II: father

Ascended to the throne: Dec 11, 1936, aged 40 years; crowned: May 12, 1937 at Westminster Abbey

Married: Elizabeth Bowes-Lyon

Children: two daughters, Elizabeth and Margaret

Died: February 6, 1952 at Sandringham, Norfolk, aged 56 years

Quotes: 'The highest of distinctions is service to others.'

Decisions made by each of the three kings – George V, Edward VIII and George VI – had influences on their own and many other people's lives: George V changed the family name, Edward VIII abdicated, and George VI sought the help of a speech therapist.
Discuss in how far their respective positions affected their decisions? To what extent were they influenced by society? And what message did their decision send to the nation?

The Windsors

GEORGE V
1865–1936

Princess Mary
1867–1953

David
DUKE OF WINDSOR
1894–1972
EDWARD VIII
(abdicated 1936)
married Wallis Simpson
(1896–1986)

Bertie
GEORGE VI
1895–1952
married Lady Elizabeth
Bowes-Lyon (Queen Elizabeth/
The Queen Mother)
(1900–2002)

Four other children:
Mary (1897–1965),
Henry (1900–1974),
George (1902–1942)
and **John** (1905–1919)

QUEEN ELIZABETH II
b. 1962
married Philip,
DUKE OF EDINBURGH

Princess Margaret
1930–2002
married Antony,
Earl of Snowdon (divorced 1978)

Charles,
Prince of Wales
b. 1984
married Lady Diana
Spencer (died 1997),
(divorced 1996)
married Camilla
Parker Bowles

Anne,
Princess Royal
b. 1950
married
Captain Mark Phillips
(divorced 1992)

Andrew,
Duke of York
b. 1960
married
Sarah Ferguson
(divorced 1996)

Edward,
Earl of Wessex
b. 1964
married
Sophie Rhys-Jones

Prince William of Wales
b. 1982
married
Catherine
Middleton

Prince Henry of Wales
b. 1984

Peter Phillips
b. 1977
married
Autumn
Kelly

Zara Phillips
b. 1981
married
Mike
Tindall

Princess Beatrice
of York
b. 1988

Princess Eugenie
of York
b. 1990

Lady Louise Windsor
b. 2003

Viscount Severn
b. 2007

The Royal Family

Work with your partner and find out more about your member of the Royal Family. Find out about their work, private life, scandals and popularity. Prepare a short presentation. You should prepare a transparency, too.

1. Queen Mum
2. Queen Elizabeth
3. Prince Philip
4. Prince Charles
5. Camilla Parker-Bowles
6. Lady Di
7. Prince William
8. Prince Harry
9. Catherine Middleton

You can use these internet sites:

- http://www.royal.gov.uk/ThecurrentRoyalFamily/Overview.aspx
- http://www.princeofwales.gov.uk/
- http://en.wikipedia.org/wiki/British_Royal_Family
- http://www.britroyals.com/.

The Royal Family – solutions

1. Queen Mum

full name: Elizabeth Angela Marguerite, née Bowes-Lyon
born 4 August 1900, grew up in Hertfordshire, was educated at home;
although she was very young, she assisted in helping the wounded of the First World War;
married the Duke of York on 26 April 1923 in Westminster Abbey; they had two children;
in 1948: Silver Wedding
activities: visited Commonwealth nations; stayed in England during the Second World War; visited badly damaged areas, hospitals, factories and troops; made several tours

2. Queen Elizabeth II

born in 1926; daughter of King George VI
full name: Elizabeth Alexandra Mary, née Windsor
was crowned at the age of 25 on 2 June 1953;
focus of public interest switched to Charles and Diana in the 1980s following "catalogue of problems" and her "annus horribilis" (term used in the Christmas message 1992); Charles and Diana get divorced; Diana's death in 1997, controversy about her late response to Diana's death;
golden jubilee in 2002; 2012 85th birthday; diamond jubilee;
she has got eight grandchildren; an animal lover since childhood, the queen is highly interested in horses; other interests include walking in the countryside, her Corgis and working her Labradors, which were bred at Sandringham; the Queen has over 600 patronages

3. Prince Philip – "The Duke of Edinburgh"

born Prince of Greece and Denmark in Corfu on 10 June 1921; evacuated from Greece by King George VI; went to school in France, Britain and Germany;
married Princess Elizabeth, daughter of George VI and heir to the throne, on 20 November 1940; four children: Prince Charles, Princess Anne, Prince Andrew, Prince Edward;
naval career: joined navy in 1929, served during World War II as well, reached rank of commander;
president of 800 organisations whose goals are: scientific and technological research; development; encouragement of sport; welfare of young people; conservation of the environment; improving British industrial life
scandals: made some odd remarks which were offensive

4. The Prince of Wales

born at 9.14 pm on 14 November 1948 at Buckingham Palace
full name: Charles Philip Arthur George
parents: Prince Philip, Duke of Edingburgh and Elizabeth II; spouses: Diana, Princess of Wales (m. 1981, div. 1996), Camilla, Duchess of Cornwall (m. 2005); earned a Bachelor of Arts; served in the Royal Navy
Charles & Diana: two sons: William (1982) and Henry (1984); divorce in 1996 because of Charles's affair with Camilla Parker-Bowles

5. Camilla Mountbatten-Windsor

born 17 July 1947 in London
full name: Camilla Rosemary, née Shand, divorced Parker-Bowles, now Mountbatten-Windsor
current holder of the titles Princess of Wales, Duchess of Cornwall, Duchess of Rothesay and Countess of Chester
4 July 1973: married Andrew Parker-Bowles; two children;
Andrew initiated divorce proceedings against Camilla, because of an extramarital affair between Charles and Camilla; affair became public knowledge as a result of a secretly recorded telephone conversation; "Camillagate, the Homeworker Scandal"; marriage between Charles and Diana broke up; Diana blamed the relationship between Charles and Camilla as the reason for the break-up of her own marriage: "Well, there were three of us in this marriage, so it was a bit crowded."
8 April 2005: married at Windsor Castle

6. Lady Di

full name: Diana Frances, née Spencer
born 1 July 1961 in Sandrinham; died 31 August 1997 as a result of a car crash in Paris
parents: Viscount and Viscountess Althorp
married Prince Charles on 29 July 1981 at St Paul's Cathedral; watched by millions in the streets and on TV; during her marriage to Prince Charles she was Princess of Wales, Duchess of Cornwall, Duchess of Rothesay, Countess of Chester, Baroness of Renfrew
two sons: William and Harry
divorce: 28 August 1996
scandals: marriage problems; affair with Major James Hewitt; publication of her biography *Diana: Her True Story* by Andrew Morton; rumours of bulimia; publication of telephone conversations; later relationship with Dodi Fayed
charities: commitment in the fields of serious illnesses like AIDS and leprosy and of young homeless or drug-addicted people; during her marriage President or Patron of more than 100 charities; supported the International Campaign to Ban Landmines

7. Prince William

full name: William Arthur Philip Louis
born 21 June 1982 in London; elder son of Prince Charles and Lady Diana
marriage to Catherine Middleton on 29 April 2011; since then: Duke of Cambridge
education: different independent schools; Eton College (geography, biology and history of art); gap year; University of St. Andrews; Royal Military Academy Sandhurst; Search and Rescue Pilot with the Royal Air Force
charities: with his brother he created the Foundation of Prince William and Prince Harry to support young people, sustainable development, and the welfare of the country's armed servicemen and women; Patron or President of further charities and organisations
scandals: landing an Air Force helicopter at the home of Kate Middleton's parents

8. Prince Harry

full name: Henry Charles Albert David
born 15 September 1984 (in London); second son of Prince Charles and Lady Di
A-levels; gap year after graduation (Australia, Argentina, Africa); in 2005 he entered the Royal Military Academy Sandhurst; in 2006 he became second lieutenant; co-founded the charity Sentebale; in 2008 two months service in the Helmand province (Afghanistan); promoted to lieutenant
scandals: snorting vodka (holiday); Swastika badge (Nazi-scandal); cannabis scandal (Eton college); racist video; posing naked in front of a camera

9. Catherine Middleton

full name: Catherine Elizabeth, née Middleton
born on 9 January 1982 in Reading
parents: Caroline and Michael Middleton
married Prince William on 29 April 2011
education: St Andrew's Prep School in Pangbourne, Berkshire and Downe House in Newbury; Marlborough College, Wiltshire; gap-year; University of St Andrews, Scotland (History of Art)
charities: Patron of the Foundation of Prince William and Prince Harry
scandals: photos of her brother James showing him naked and in women's clothes

How well do you know the Royal Family?

Fill in the gaps.

George VI was the son of ______________________ of Teck and her husband ______________________ V. Apart from Albert, the later George VI, whose family nickname was ______________________, the couple had ______________________ other children, including ______________________, who became King in 1936 and John, who died as a child. Edward VIII was never crowned, as he abdicated in ______________________ because he wanted to marry ______________________, a twice-divorced American. Edward's younger brother ______________________ ascended to the throne in ______________________. He had two daughters with his wife ______________________, named ______________________ and ______________________. ______________________ is now the Queen of England.

Solutions:
Mary, George, Bertie, four, David, 1936, Wallis Simpson, Albert, 1936, Elizabeth, Elizabeth, Margaret, Elizabeth

Introducing a prince's life – first scene of the film

1. Watch the scene. Take notes on the actions and sounds during your first viewing, take notes on the camera operations during your second viewing.

	1st viewing		2nd viewing
	action	sound	camera
before the speech • BBC news reader • Bertie			
during the speech			

2. Describe the atmosphere that is created.

____

____

____

3. What is the function of the scene?

____

____

____

The King's Speech – royal life

1. Take notes on Bertie's and Elizabeth's life with regard to different aspects.

aspects	life of a Royal Highness	camera operations/setting
living conditions		
language		
children		
duties		
other aspects		

2. What is the function of the scene?

The King's Speech – a commoner's life

1. Take notes on Lionel's life with regard to different aspects.

aspects	life of a commoner	camera operations/setting
living conditions		
language		
children		
duties		
other aspects		

2. What is the function of the scene?

Component 3

My game, my rules, my turf – speech therapy

In diesem *Component* wird der inhaltliche Schwerpunkt dem Stottern und den im Film dargestellten Therapieansätzen gewidmet. Es wird erneut deutlich, wie überraschend, untypisch und weitreichend Logues Rolle im Leben von Bertie war, da er als *commoner* ohne Kontakte, Empfehlungen und Diplome ohne die unkonventionellen Schritte von Elizabeth seinem prominenten Patienten niemals begegnet wäre, der weiterhin von Günstlingen des Hofes wie Sir Blandine-Bentham oder anderen altherkömmlichen Behandlungsmethoden ausgeliefert gewesen wäre.
Zu Beginn soll daher der im Palast stattfindende Therapieversuch mit Zigaretten und Murmeln analysiert werden, um die Ergebnisse anschließend mit Logues erstem Auftreten zu vergleichen.
Die inhaltlichen Aspekte wie der Behandlungsansatz von Sir Blandine-Bentham und Berties und Elizabeths Reaktionen darauf sollen hier wiederum komplettiert werden durch die Analyse der *cinematic devices*.

3.1 Sir Blandine-Bentham: Speech therapy?

In der Szene, in der Bertie von Sir Blandine-Bentham be- bzw. misshandelt wird, werden einerseits die Eindrücke eines von starren Regeln und Hierarchien geprägten Lebens der Mitglieder der königlichen Familie bestätigt, andererseits jedoch auch die Scharlatanerie kritisiert, die innerhalb dieser Schicht florieren konnte (Lionel fasst das in der folgenden Szene in seiner ersten Sitzung mit Bertie zusammen, indem er die Ärzte, die das Rauchen empfohlen haben, als Idioten kritisiert und Berties Einwand „They've all been knighted." mit „Makes it official then." abtut.). Um den Kontrast zwischen den beiden Therapeuten herauszuarbeiten, wird in diesem ersten Schritt Sir Blandine-Benthams wenig hilfreiches, aber umso autoritäreres Auftreten analysiert, das von den *camera works* besonders gut unterstrichen wird.

German DVD
0:05:21 – 0:07:35

English DVD
0:04:53 – 0:06:43

Die Schülerinnen und Schüler schauen die Szene erst unter inhaltlichen Aspekten an (Arbeitsaufträge 1 – 3) und konzentrieren sich anschließend auf die filmischen Mittel, mit denen sie ihre zuvor gewonnenen Eindrücke belegen können (Arbeitsauftrag 4). Abschließend wird die Funktion dieser Szene im Kontext des Films kurz zusammengefasst.

1. Describe both Sir Blandine-Bentham's speech therapy and Bertie's and Elizabeth's reactions to it!
2. Why does Bertie – to your mind – react like this?
3. What impression do you get of Elizabeth?
4. Note down striking cinematic devices in the scene and their effects.
5. Note down the function of the scene.

Die Ergebnisse dieser Erarbeitungsphase können anschließend im Unterrichtsgespräch in einem Tafelbild zusammengefasst werden (**Lösungsvorschlag/möglicher Tafelanschrieb**):

therapy	Sir Blandine-Bentham is an old man, flattered because is consulted, devout, his **therapy** consists of strange, old fashioned methods like cigarettes and marbles		low-angle shots → powerful position	**cinematic devices**
reactions	**Bertie:** • smokes • looks sceptical but stuffs marbles into his mouth – does not succeed and must spit them out • starts swearing	**Elizabeth:** • looks up when the doctor suggests that Bertie should smoke • during the marble therapy she looks interested and asks questions	close-up shots → Bertie is smoking, cannot speak, strained face close-up of marbles → seem threateningly big high-angle shots of Bertie from the doctor's perspective → Bertie appears small and helpless eye-level shot of Elizabeth → self-confident	
reasons	• reacts angrily and testily because anger is his way of dealing with problems. • is disappointed with himself and desperate → rage is his means of letting off steam.	• is very supportive, but also sceptical → questions Sir Blandine-Bentham's old-fashioned methods		
The **function** of this scene is to show why Bertie refuses more therapy and to explain why the treatment and the relationship between him and Lionel Logue begin on such bad terms. This scene will provide stark contrast to Lionel's methods and techniques.				

3.2 Lionel Logue: Speech therapy!

Bevor der folgende Filmausschnitt mit dem ersten Auftritt von Lionel Logue in seiner Praxis gezeigt wird, sollen die Schülerinnen und Schüler sich in die Lage des Ehepaares Bertie und Elizabeth versetzen, die nach der erniedrigenden Therapiesitzung und dem Wutausbruch Berties nun unterschiedliche Interessen haben: Bertie möchte nie wieder von einem Sprachtherapeuten behandelt werden, aber Elizabeth sieht, dass ein Leben ohne Sprachstörung, besonders in seiner Position, wesentlich einfacher sein wird, sodass für sie nur ein Wechsel der Therapieform infrage kommt. Ausgehend von dieser Situation entwerfen die Schülerinnen und Schüler nun einen Dialog, in dem wesentliche Grundsätze des *negotiating* eingeübt und eingehalten werden sollen. Die fünf Tipps des *negotiating* können entweder vorher thematisiert oder der Lerngruppe in kopierter Form mit der Aufgabenstellung gegeben werden. Die Ausgestaltung in Form eines Rollenspiels kann entweder in Partnerarbeit erfolgen oder in Dreiergruppen, in denen die Rollen wechseln und der dritte Schüler jeweils eine Beobachterrolle einnimmt und Verbesserungsvorschläge einbringt.

Negotiating: Therapies?!

Elizabeth and Bertie argue about further treatment. One of you assumes the role of Bertie who is complaining about the therapy and who flatly refuses any more treatment, and the other one is Elizabeth, the 'negotiator'.

Act out the situation and try to come to an amicable solution. If this isn't possible, try to ensure that Bertie understands Elizabeth's view of the situation.

Tips for your negotiating skills

1. Listen attentively!
   To show the other person that you are listening you can repeat what has just been said. At the same time this allows you to control the course of the conversation.
2. Stay calm!
   Sometimes personal feelings are involved and people get hurt or aggressive. You have to stay calm and should not let your emotions rule the conversation. A short break or a step back in the chronology of the conversation helps to relax the atmosphere.
3. Make a deal!
   Finding a solution is essential, but you have to make sure that you can live with the compromise, i.e. your suggestions have to be realistic.
4. Offer something!
   Tell the other person what you can do to improve or solve the situation. If you can only offer small changes, you can focus on these positive aspects ("Unfortunately I can't promise you a complete change/a direct solution, but what I can do now is…").
5. Be clear!
   You should not give in when you feel that the demand is impossible. Explain why you can't do this so that the other person can understand your point of view.

Kontrastiv zu der unglücklich verlaufenden Therapiesitzung, in der Sir Blandine-Bentham stellvertretend für die den Thronfolger umgebende prätentiöse Gesellschaft mit ihrem Dünkel steht, sollen nun die erste Begegnung zwischen Elizabeth und Lionel Logue sowie das Aufeinandertreffen von Bertie und Logue im Rahmen ihrer ersten, Behandlung betrachtet werden. Das Augenmerk der Schülerinnen und Schüler sollte im ersten Teil (Frage 1) vor allem auf der Person Logues und seiner Praxis liegen, um den Therapeuten selbst und die vorherrschende Atmosphäre möglichst gut mit der zuvor behandelten Szene vergleichen zu können. Auffallend ist die ruhige Autorität, die Logue ausstrahlt und mit der er sogar seine „Vorgänger", die Ärzte, die Bertie bisher behandelt haben, als „idiots" bezeichnet und den Einwand von Bertie („They've all been knighted.") mit äußerster Selbstsicherheit abtut („Makes it official then.").
Die Beobachtungsaufgaben für die Schülerinnen und Schüler sind analog zu denen der Behandlung durch Sir Blandine-Bentham, sodass auch die beiden Tafelbilder zur besseren Übersicht nebeneinander angeordnet werden können.

German DVD
0:17:24–0:28:22

English DVD
0:16:56–0:27:47

1. Describe the speech therapist Lionel Logue and his practice. What is your first impression?
2. Describe Lionel's therapy and Bertie's reaction.
3. What impression do you get of Lionel both as a person and as a speech therapist?
4. Note down striking cinematic devices in the scene and their effects.
5. Note down the function of the scene.

Lösungsvorschlag/möglicher Tafelanschrieb (Folie):

<table>
<tr>
<td>therapy</td>
<td colspan="2">• Lionel wants to build rapport by offering tea and making small talk.
• He treats his patients as equal partners.
• He wants to talk about Bertie's past, which is part of psychotherapy.
• By making jokes and bets Lionel dares his patient and tries to bring him out of his shell.
• He owns the latest devices used for speech therapy, e. g. a speech recorder with whose help he is able to record Bertie's voice on a disc.
• Being honest is part of Lionel's therapy: he openly tells Bertie that he thinks he has a temper.
↓
Lionel seems to be a modern, open-minded and competent person who knows what he's doing (new methods).</td>
<td>medium shots to create a formal atmosphere and to allow the viewer to see the actors' body language.</td>
<td>cinematic devices</td>
</tr>
<tr>
<td></td>
<td colspan="2">↙ ↘</td>
<td></td>
<td></td>
</tr>
<tr>
<td>reactions</td>
<td>Bertie:
• He does not want any tea and is not interested in conversation but in actions and therapy.
• He seems sceptical and does not want to be treated as an equal by a commoner.
• However, he answers Lionel's questions.
• He reacts in a choleric manner when asked about his past as he does not want to discuss personal matters.
• He is sceptical with regard to Lionel's jokes and the gramophone, but he tries the recording anyway and gets really angry and refuses further therapy when he thinks he is not reading properly.</td>
<td>Elizabeth:
• startled by the unusual approach
• convinced by Logue's self-confident manner</td>
<td>establishing shot when Bertie looks around;
eye-level medium shots when they talk to each other to stress equality;
Logue's calm friendliness creates a pleasant atmosphere although Bertie does not want to relax;
music when Bertie's voice is recorded to surprise the audience in a later scene</td>
<td>cinematic devices</td>
</tr>
<tr>
<td>reasons</td>
<td>• As before, he reacts angrily and testily because anger is his way of dealing with problems.
• He has a low frustration tolerance level.
• Lionel's methods seem to be too strange for Bertie.</td>
<td>• is very supportive</td>
<td></td>
<td></td>
</tr>
<tr>
<td colspan="5">→ The function of this scene is to introduce a new, strange kind of speech therapy that constitutes a contrast to Sir Blandine-Bentham's therapy and to show Bertie's scepticism after having undergone various different and sometimes humiliating forms of treatment.</td>
</tr>
</table>

Neben den *viewing skills* und dem oben erwähnten *negotiating* ist das Verfassen von Beschwerdebriefen – auch oder gerade in englischer Sprache – im alltäglichen Leben von großer Bedeutung, sodass auch dieser *skill* im Englischunterricht eingeübt werden sollte. Es ist anzunehmen, dass den Schülerinnen und Schülern Lionel Logue sehr sympathisch erscheint, aber es wird in dem zuvor behandelten Filmauszug auch deutlich, dass dieser positive Eindruck von Bertie nicht geteilt wird, der sich unangemessen behandelt fühlt und sich die Zutraulichkeiten eines normalen Bürgerlichen verbittet. Diese negativen Eindrücke sollen nun in einem *formal letter of complaint* ausgedrückt werden, der aus der Perspektive des Duke of York nach dieser ersten Sitzung geschrieben wird. Diese Aufgabe erfordert einerseits Empathie für Bertie und andererseits eine aufmerksame Bestandsaufnahme seiner Reaktionen auf Logue, sodass eventuell ein erneutes Sehen der Szene notwendig ist.
Hilfestellungen können den Schülerinnen und Schülern in Form der *Tips for writing letters of complaint* an die Hand gegeben werden.

German DVD
0:17:24–0:28:22

English DVD
0:16:56–0:27:47

Having abruptly left the first therapy lesson with Lionel Logue, Bertie is still furious about Logue's impertinent manner. He wants to vent his anger and writes a letter of complaint.
Write his letter. Pay special attention to using formal language and form.

Tips for writing letters of complaint

1. Write a formal letter!
   The tone must be formal or neutral (and not aggressive or insulting, as this does not encourage the person reading the letter to solve the problem). Either begin with the person's name (*Dear Mr X/Dear Ms X*) or, if you want to write to a company, with *Dear Sir/Madam*. End your letter *Yours faithfully* and sign your name.
2. Describe the situation!
   You start by describing the background of your complaint. You can use phrases like "I am writing to inform you of my dissatisfaction with…" or "I am writing to complain about…".
3. Describe the problem!
   Clearly state what caused the problem and, if possible, which negative effects this has for you. The letter has to contain enough details to avoid further questions.
4. Offer a solution!
   Say what you want to happen. You might just want to express your disappointment, or you may want a letter of apology or a refund ("I am writing to ask you to please correct/change/send…").
5. Ask for a reply!
   You should tell the other person that you expect a reply ("I look forward to receiving your reply.").

Nachdem, aufgrund des zeitlichen Umfangs am besten in einer Hausaufgabe, Beschwerdebriefe verfasst wurden, können in der darauffolgenden Stunde entsprechende Antwortschreiben verfasst werden. Die Briefe werden innerhalb der Lerngruppe ausgetauscht, sodass jede Schülerin und jeder Schüler ein Anschreiben hat, auf das eine Erwiderung verschriftlicht werden muss. Hier ist es wichtig, auf die genannten Aspekte einzugehen, aber dabei die Perspektive von Lionel Logue einzunehmen, der sich wahrscheinlich nicht auf den förmlichen Ton des Duke of York einlassen, sondern mit „Dear Bertie" und in einem auf seinem bisherigen Herangehen insistierenden Ton antworten wird.

Um den im Filmausschnitt gewonnenen subjektiven Eindruck von Logues ruhiger und professioneller Ausstrahlung zu untermauern, kann nun ein Text aus *Medical News Today* von Christian Nordquist ("What is Stammering, Stuttering?", ***Copy 16***) eingesetzt werden, der das Phänomen des Stotterns ebenso wie mögliche Therapien grundlegend erläutert und die im Film zu beobachtenden Symptome, die Bertie beim Stottern zeigt, sowie Logues Behandlungsmethoden mit bemerkenswerten Übereinstimmungen zusammenfassend darstellt.

Lösungsvorschlag zu *Copy 16:*

1. Stammering is a hesitation or stop in the speech or a prolongation of certain sounds. It can be accompanied by physical symptoms such as blinking, tapping, or tensing up.
   Stammering decreases when the person is relaxed and calm. Stress, pressure, unfamiliar situations and listener's impatience often aggravate the problems.
2. Nearly all the symptoms can be detected in the film. Surprisingly, Logue already uses many of the accepted treatments: controlled breathing; stretching certain sounds; identifying situations/feelings/attitudes; "cancellations", "pull-outs" and "preparatory sets"; practising special sounds (e.g. the tongue-twisters).

Im Rahmen der zweiten Aufgabe bietet es sich an, die einzelnen Aspekte in einem weiterführenden Schritt nicht nur auf der inhaltlichen Ebene, sondern auch hinsichtlich filmischer Darstellungsweisen zu untersuchen, da die Szenen des Stotterns und der Therapiesitzungen diesbezüglich viele Einsichten bieten. Durch die schauspielerische Leistung von Colin Firth wird das Leiden bereits in der ersten Rede im Wembley Stadion realistisch herausgestellt. Die Erstbegegnung von Bertie und Logue wurde zu Beginn dieses *Components* unter allgemeineren Aspekten untersucht, sodass die Schülerinnen und Schüler ihre Beobachtungen nun ergänzen und anhand von weiteren Szenen vervollständigen können. Eine der Therapiesitzungen ist als Klausurvorschlag (**Klausur 1**) enthalten, sodass diese Szene gegebenenfalls als Beispiel an dieser Stelle ausgespart werden sollte.

3.3 The history of speech therapy

Die Behandlung von Sprachstörungen hat sich im Lauf der Jahre verändert und weiterentwickelt, so dass es neben den bereits angesprochenen bzw. gezeigten Methoden von der Antike bis heute viele verschiedene und unterschiedlich erfolgreiche Ansätze gab. Hier bietet sich die Möglichkeit zu weitreichender Recherchearbeit, eventuell für einzelne Schülerinnen oder Schüler, die entweder mithilfe des Internets oder Bibliotheken oder aber durch einen Besuch bei einem Logopäden Informationen sammeln, die als Referat der Lerngruppe präsentiert werden, wobei entsprechende *presentation skills* eingeübt werden.

Tips for your presentation skills

1. Guide your audience!
   Start with a clear introduction that contains three major aspects: 1. the reason for the presentation, 2. the topic, 3. the time you will need.
2. Structure your presentation!
   A clearly structured main body of presentation makes it more memorable. Organising your ideas into groups of three (as in the introduction) helps the

audience to focus on what you say. Include only aspects that are relevant to your listeners and your objective and exclude all other information.

3. Summarize the main ideas!
   At the end you should mention your main aspects in a short conclusion and invite the audience to ask questions.

4. Speak freely!
   When giving your presentation, you must be familiar with the subject so that you do not have to read a text. You can use notes (keywords) on small cards to help you if you get lost, but when you have prepared your presentation well, you might not even need them. Additionally, speaking freely enables to you establish eye contact with the members of your audience and to use appropriate body language/gestures.

5. Rehearse!
   Before giving your presentation in front of an audience, you should practise it!

6. Use visual aids!
   Visual aids help your audience to remember what you are saying. You can use pictures, posters, slides, graphs, charts… but do not use too many or put too much information into them – and give your audience time to look at them and understand them.

Das Beispiel von King George VI, der sich seinem Stottern und den damit verbundenen Hemmungen und Beeinträchtigungen gestellt und sie damit überwunden hat, lädt ein, weitere berühmte Persönlichkeiten zu suchen, die in ihrem Leben entweder eine Sprachstörung oder ein anders geartetes Hindernis überwunden haben. Zu ersteren zählen z. B. Aristoteles, Elvis Presley, Bruce Willis oder Rowan Atkinson, bei letzteren lassen sich so diverse Personen wie beispielsweise der mittlerweile fast vollständig gelähmte Physiker Stephen Hawking, die australische Surferin Bethany Hamilton, die durch einen Haiangriff ihren linken Arm verlor, oder die blinden Sänger Stevie Wonder oder Andrea Bocelli nennen. Die große Bandbreite der hier nur exemplarisch aufgeführten Menschen lässt ahnen, dass ein genauerer Blick in ihren Alltag und den Umgang mit ihrer Behinderung äußerst interessant ist. Hier bietet es sich an, die Schülerinnen und Schüler in einem *Brainstorming* ihnen bekannte Personen zusammentragen bzw. in einer Hausaufgabe recherchieren und eine Biografie wählen zu lassen, die sie interessiert.

Zusammenfassende Internetseiten sind z. B.:
- http://www.disabled-world.com/artman/publish/article_0060.shtml
- http://hcdg.org/famous.htm

Christian Nordqvist: What Is Stammering, Stuttering?

Stammering and stuttering have the same meaning – it is a speech disorder in which the person repeats or prolongs words, syllables or phrases. The person with a stutter (or stammer) may also stop during speech and make no sound for certain syllables. People who stutter often find that stress and fatigue make it harder for them to talk flowingly, as well as situations in which they become self-conscious about speaking, such as public speaking or teaching. Most people who stutter find that their problem eases if they are relaxed. […]
Stuttering is common when children are learning to speak. However, the majority of kids grow out of this stage of initial stuttering. For some, however, the problem persists and requires some kind of professional help, such as speech therapy. It is important that parents do not add to a child's stress by drawing too much attention to the problem when they are trying to communicate verbally. The calmer a child feels the less acute the symptoms tend to become.

What are the signs and symptoms of stuttering?

- Problems starting a word, phrase or sentence
- Hesitation before certain sounds have to be uttered
- Repeating a sound, word or syllable
- Certain speech sounds may be prolonged
- Speech may come out in spurts
- Words with certain sounds are substituted for others (circumlocution)
- Rapid blinking (when trying to talk)
- Trembling lips (when trying to talk)
- Foot may tap (when trying to talk)
- Trembling jaw (when trying to talk)
- Face and/or upper body tighten up (when trying to talk)
- Some may appear out of breath when talking
- Interjection, such as "uhm" used more frequently before attempting to utter certain sounds […]

in spurts very suddenly and quickly

What is the treatment for stuttering?

A good evaluation (diagnosis) is vital as this determines what the best treatment might be. Treatments for people who stutter tend to be aimed at teaching the person skills, strategies, and behaviors that help oral communication. This may include:

Controlling monitoring speech rate – this may involve practicing smooth, fluent speech at very slow speed, using short sentences and phrases. The person is taught to stretch vowels and consonants, while trying to secure continuous airflow. With practice the person gradually utters smooth speech at higher speed, and with longer sentences and phrases. Patients have higher long-term success rates if the sessions with the SLP are followed up regularly – this helps prevent relapses.

practicing AE
practising BE

Breathing control – as the patient practices prolonged speech he/she also learns how to regulate breathing. Added to this is operant conditioning (controlling breathing, as well as phonation, and articulation (lips, jaw and tongue).

practice AE
practise BE

Stuttering modification therapy
The aim here is to modify the stuttering so that it is easier and requires less of an effort, rather than eliminating it. This therapy works on the principle that if anxiety exacerbates stuttering, using easier stuttering with less avoidance and fear will alleviate the stuttering. Charles Van Riper developed ***Block Modification Therapy*** in 1973; it includes four stages:

to exacerbate to make worse

Stage 1 (Identification) – the therapist and the patient identify the core behaviors, secondary behaviors, and feelings and attitudes that accompany the stuttering.

Stage 2 (Desensitization) – the patient freezes stuttering behavior in an attempt to reduce fear and anxiety – this involves confronting difficult sounds, words and situations (rather than avoiding them), and stuttering intentionally (voluntary stuttering).

Stage 3 (Modification) – the patient learns *easy stuttering*. He/she learns how to apply: a) 'cancellations' – stopping a dysfluency, pausing for a moment, and then repeating the word, b) 'pull-outs' – pulling out of a dysfluency into fluent speech, c) and 'preparatory sets' – anticipating words that cause stuttering and using 'easy stuttering' on those words.

Stage 4 (Stabilization) – the patient prepares practice assignments, makes preparatory sets and pull-outs automatic, and changes the way he/she sees himself/herself from being a stutterer to being a person who speaks fluently most of the time, but stutters mildly occasionally. [...]

http://www.medicalnewstoday.com [14 02 2013]

1. What is stammering? What alleviates and what aggravates the symptoms?
2. Looking at various scenes from the film, find out which of the manifestations mentioned here Bertie suffers from and which elements of the above-mentioned forms of treatment are used by Logue.

Component 4

Family relations

In diesem *Component* wird der inhaltliche Schwerpunkt den familiären Beziehungen gewidmet. Es wird deutlich, wie autoritär und wenig verständnisvoll Bertie von seinem Vater George V behandelt wurde. Dies ist ein möglicher Erklärungsansatz für Berties Stottern und sein geringes Selbstvertrauen. Ferner ermöglicht das problematische Verhältnis zu seinem Vater ein vertieftes Verständnis von Berties Bedürfnis, alles richtig zu machen und ein vorbildliches Mitglied der *Royal Family* zu sein.

Die folgenden Arbeitsblätter dienen auch dazu, Davids Problematik zu beleuchten. David, der sich wenig für Politik und seine Pflichten interessiert, wird nach dem Tod seines Vaters in eine Rolle gezwängt, die nicht zu ihm passt.

Die Analyse der Szene in Lionels Praxis nach dem Tod des Königs zeigt, wie Bertie sich zum ersten Mal Lionel anvertraut und über seine schwierige Kindheit berichtet. Der Zuschauer versteht nun besser, wie es zu Berties Sprachbehinderung kommen konnte. Der Vergleich mit der Kindheit von Berties Tochter Elizabeth verdeutlicht, dass Bertie im Gegensatz zu ihr nie auf seine Rolle als König vorbereitet wurde.

In der anschließenden Szene auf *Balmoral Castle* zeigt sich, dass Edward VIII Wallis wichtiger als sein Thron ist und dass ein Konflikt zwischen den Brüdern entsteht.

Ganz am Ende des *Components* sollen sich die Schüler mithilfe der *Hot-Seat*-Methode noch einmal in beide Charaktere versetzen, da beide innerlich zerrissen sind: Edward zwischen der Krone und Wallis, Bertie zwischen der Treue zu seinem Bruder und der Liebe zu seinem Land.

4.1 Bertie and his father

German DVD
0:28:23–0:31:48

English DVD
0:27:55–0:31:19

Im Rahmen der Szene an Weihnachten in *Sandrigham Castle* bietet es sich an, den Filmausschnitt zweimal zu zeigen, sodass die Schüler sich sowohl inhaltliche als auch filmtechnische Notizen machen können, um für die Klausur zu üben. Der Einsatz dieser Szene dient nicht nur der Herausarbeitung des Verhältnisses zwischen George V und Bertie, sondern auch der Vorausdeutung, dass David der Rolle des Königs nicht gewachsen sein wird.

Als Ergänzung in einem Leistungskurs oder weiterführende Hausaufgabe bietet sich der Briefausschnitt aus dem Brief König Georges anlässlich Berties fünftem Geburtstag an, da auch hier deutlich wird, wie streng George V als Vater war und wie wichtig ihm Disziplin und Gehorsam waren. Dieses authentische Textmaterial am Ende von ***Copy 17*** bestätigt den im Film gewonnenen Eindruck.

Lösungsvorschlag zu *Copy 17*:

1. Bertie's father is very dominant, he tells him what to do by using imperatives. Bertie tries to please his father but is not successful.
2. Bertie is filmed from a high angle and is father is filmed from a low angle. Further question: Can you draw a conclusion between Bertie's relationship to his father and his character? Low self-esteem?

3. The Royal Family have become actors who must invade homes instead of just looking good in uniforms.
4. Herr Hitler is intimidating half of Europe and Marshall Stalin the other half.
5. The function of the scene is to show that Bertie's relationship to his father might be one reason for his stammering and to hint at the fact that David will not make a good king (foreshadowing).
6. Duty is very important to Bertie as he tries to fulfil all the tasks that come his way as prince and King. Bertie tries to please his father and is very disappointed in himself when he fails, as can be seen when he isn't able to read the Christmas Broadcast at Sandringham Castle.

4.2 David and his father

Bevor im nächsten Schritt auf das Verhältnis von David und King George V eingegangen wird, folgt in der Chronologie des Films erst die zweite Therapiesitzung bei Lionel Logue. Diese wird hier jedoch nicht thematisiert, da sie Inhalt des Klausurvorschlags ist.
Die folgende Hintergrundinformation (siehe *Box*) zu der Besonderheit der Zeitumstellung in *Sandringham Castle* bietet sich als vorbereitenden Hausaufgabe, Internetrecherche oder alternativ als Lehrervortrag oder Mini-Schülerreferat an, da die im Film gezeigte Szene, in der David kurz vor dem Tod seines Vaters die Uhr in Schloss Sandringham umstellt, ohne diesen Kontext nicht verstanden wird.

Background information: "Sandringham Time"

Edward VII established the custom of keeping every clock at Sandringham Castle, the royal residence, half an hour fast in order to be able to rise earlier and enjoy the best shooting conditions. George V had stuck to his father's idea and Edward VIII (David) changes the time to GMT (Greenwich Mean Time) in a rage, as can be seen in the film when George V is ill.

Im Anschluss an die letzte Szene, in der George V als dominanter und weitsichtiger Vater porträtiert wurde, folgt nun die Analyse der Szene, in der er stirbt und sein als Lebemann dargestellter erster Sohn David ihm auf den Thron folgt. George V ist nun geistig verwirrt und völlig hilflos, ganz im Gegensatz zur vorherigen Szene.

The King's Speech – The King is dead, long live the King

German DVD
0:37:24–0:44:05

English DVD
0:36:57–0:43:34

1. Describe the impression you get of David (Edward VIII).
2. Note down how King George V is portrayed in this particular scene.
3. Note down the moment in which "Sandringham Time" is mentioned.
4. Why does Archbishop Lang talk to David during dinner?
5. Note down David's reactions after his father's death.
6. Note down the function of the scene

Lösungsvorschlag:

1. David seems to be a cool playboy as he is dressed in a leather jacket and arrives by plane. One gets the impression that David is conceited and self-

centred as he thinks his father became ill voluntarily to complicate his relationship with Wallis Simpson ("The old man is doing this on purpose"). David is henpecked as he is always on the phone with Wallis excusing himself.

2. George V is confused and seems weak and seeks help. He cannot act the King anymore and is portrayed differently as in the last scene with Bertie in Sandringham. This is also displayed in the different camera angles that are used this time.
3. David is late for dinner and angry. That is why he changes the time.
4. Archbishop Lang is ingratiating himself with David and tries to befriend him as he knows that George V will die.
5. David starts to cry and runs away. He says: "Poor Wallis, I'm trapped."
6. The function is to show the conflict David is experiencing.

Als weiterführende Aspekte im Anschluss an die Besprechung der Ergebnisse bieten sich folgende Fragen an:

Why is David so desperate after his father's death?
What would you do if you were Bertie?

In der Diskussion der ersten Frage könnten verschiedene Meinungen geäußert werden, warum David auf den Tod seines Vaters so heftig reagiert. Zum einen ist er über den Verlust seines Vaters erschüttert, zum anderen verzweifelt über die Folgen, die dessen Tod mit sich bringen wird. Um die Frage endgültig zu klären, dient ein Einblick in die Biografie Georges VI, der Aufschluss darüber liefert, dass David sich in seiner Rolle als Thronfolger gefangen fühlte. Die folgende Informationsbox könnte den Schülern vorgelesen oder als Informationstext ausgeteilt werden.

Background information on George V's death

Prince Albert, who had been closest of all the brothers to his father, must have been surprised at his elder brother's extreme reaction to his father's death. Just before King George died, the Prince of Wales [...] became hysterical, cried loudly, and kept on embracing the Queen [and when death had arrived he] left the room crying aloud [...]. Prince Albert could not know that the hysteria was caused by panic; his brother was locked in a personal crisis made far more difficult for him to resolve now that his father was dead. Edward VIII's household came to believe that he had intended to elope with Wallis before his father died, thus resolving the situation with a *fait accompli.* [...] A note written three weeks before his father's death by the Prince of Wales to Wallis on New Year's Day 1936 seems to indicate that this was, indeed, what he was contemplating ('Oh! my Wallis I know we'll have Viel Gluck [sic!] to make us one this year'). But as King he could not so easily do what as Prince of Wales he could have done, and was probably envisaging doing: marry Wallis and give up his rights to the succession. He had left it too late and now the trap had closed on him.

Die Frage, was die Schülerinnen und Schüler hingegen nun an Berties Stelle tun würden, könnte folgendermaßen beantwortet werden:

talk to a friend, talk to Elizabeth, talk to a family member etc.

Im Film wendet sich Bertie tatsächlich dann an Lionel, den einzigen Mann, der ihm in dieser Situation zuverlässig erscheint und der der Stellung eines Freundes trotz aller Differenzen am nächsten kommt, und sucht ihn auf, um über den Tod seines Vaters zu sprechen.

Da sowohl David als auch Bertie in dieser Szene sehr aufgewühlt sind, kann die im Film vorhandene Leerstelle idealerweise für eine kreative Aufgabe genutzt werden. Die Schüler sollen sich entweder in der Stunde oder als Hausaufgabe in einen der beiden Charaktere versetzen und einen Tagebucheintrag am Todestag ihres Vaters verfassen. Eine solche kreative Aufgabe schult das Einfühlungsvermögen und stellt eine gezielte Vorbereitung für das Zentralabitur dar. Falls diese Textsorte noch nicht eingeübt wurde, kann die Tool Box als Folie oder Arbeitsblatt verwendet werden.

Write the diary entry Bertie/David would have written after his father's death. Don't forget the rules of a diary entry.

How to write a diary entry

There are no fixed rules for diary entries as they are individual. Nevertheless, there are some guidelines for diary entries:

1. **The Greeting** Start your diary with "Dear Diary" or give the diary a name
2. **The First Person Perspective**
3. **Secrets** In a diary you write about things you would never tell anyone else.
4. **Feelings & Thoughts** You impart your deepest thoughts and feelings.
5. **Adjectives/Adverbs** Use them to make your text more lively.
6. **Final Words** Close your diary entry with a final phrase

Don't forget that you can use informal language, e.g. short forms and colloquial language as the relationship to a diary is very close.

4.3 Bertie's childhood

In der nächsten Unterrichtseinheit wird die Szene in Lionels Praxis am Tag nach dem Tod von Berties Vater analysiert (*Bertie's childhood*), um zum einen mehr über Berties Kindheit und zum anderen über sein Verhältnis zu David zu erfahren (siehe Aufgaben 4.5). Hier bietet sich darüber hinaus der oben schon erwähnte Vergleich mit der Kindheit von Berties Tochter Elisabeth, der heutigen *Queen*, an. Zur Vorbereitung auf die Klausur dienen sowohl ein Text als auch eine Filmszene als Grundlage. Der Text wird auf ***Copy 18*** zur Verfügung gestellt. Dieser Schritt dient dazu, Berties Kindheit mit der von *Queen Elizabeth II* zu vergleichen und Unterschiede zu erkennen. Ferner wird durch die Frage nach dem Verhältnis zu David Konfliktpotenzial deutlich. Dies dient als Vorbereitung für den Streit der Brüder über Wallis Simpson in der nachfolgenden Szene in *Balmoral Castle*.
Zunächst sehen die Schülerinnen und Schüler die Filmszene und bearbeiten folgende Aufgaben:

German DVD
0:45:35–0:54:03

English DVD
0:45:06–0:53:35

Aufgaben zur Filmszene: Bertie visits Lionel after his father's death

1. Take down notes on Bertie's childhood.
2. Sum up what Bertie tells Lionel about his brother David.

Lösungsvorschlag:

1. Bertie had to collect stamps as his father didn't allow other hobbies, like building aeroplanes. Furthermore, Bertie was teased during his childhood and sometimes his father encouraged this teasing. Bertie used to be closest to nannies and his father wanted his children to be afraid of him as he himself had feared his father. Although he was left-handed, Bertie was trained to use his right hand instead and his knock-knees were corrected by wearing metal splints day and night, which was very painful. One of the nannies preferred David and didn't give Bertie enough to eat hence he still suffers from stomach problems. This nanny pinched him so that he was given back to her when the children were presented to their parents once a day. Bertie didn't have real friends and suffered when his brother Johnny died from epilepsy.
2. Bertie and David were close and David was very helpful in arranging introductions to women. On the other hand, David teased him.

Anschließend wird der Text (***Copy 18***) gelesen und inhaltlich zusammengefasst (Aufgabe 1). Das Verhältnis zwischen Elizabeth II und ihrem Vater wird im Gegensatz zum Verhältnis zwischen George V und seinem Sohn Bertie als sehr liebevoll dargestellt. Elizabeth wusste ferner schon als 12-Jährige, dass sie ihrem Vater nach dessen Tod auf den Thron folgen würde und wurde ab dem Teenageralter auf ihre Rolle als zukünftige Königin vorbereitet, was sich für sie – im Vergleich mit dem Werdegang ihres Vaters – als großer Vorteil erwies. Die Tatsache, dass Elizabeth während des Krieges in Abwesenheit ihrer Eltern die Rolle des *head of state* innehatte, ist für Oberstufenschüler, die etwa in diesem Alter sind, besonders überraschend. In einem weiteren Schritt werden dann diese Erkenntnisse mit den Ergebnissen der zuvor gesehenen Filmszene bzw. mit Kenntnissen weiterer Aspekte des Films verglichen.

Aufgaben zum Text: Her Majesty Queen Elizabeth II *(Copy 18)*

1. Sum up what Elizabeth's childhood was like according to the text.
2. Compare Bertie's and Elizabeth's upbringing regarding their preparation for being a sovereign and give evidence from what you have seen so far in the film.

Lösungsvorschlag:

1. Elizabeth was interested in horses. Despite being educated at home, she received constitutional history lessons at Eton. Elizabeth had always been interested in history. Her carefree childhood ended when she was 11. Elizabeth's attitude then changed to a more mature, responsible attitude towards life and duty. Elizabeth was born a natural leader.
2. From the age of 11 on, Elizabeth was prepared to become the next Queen, whereas Bertie was not. He had never had any preparation. He just had to deliver some speeches in his role as the Duke of York. Thus, when he was older, he had some speech therapy, but as he was not the Prince of Wales he had never expected to become King.

4.4 Wallis Simpson

Als nächstes bietet es sich an, die Figur der Wallis Simpson genauer zu betrachten. Um diesen Charakter ranken viele Mythen und auch heute fasziniert die zweifach geschiedene Frau, die dem Thronfolger den Kopf verdreht und ihn zur Abdankung motiviert hat, die Medien und viele Menschen. Da sie im Film *The King's Speech* als Person zum ersten Mal als Gastgeberin einer Party in Balmoral auftaucht, auf der es zu einem Streit zwischen David und Edward kommt, liegt es nahe, zwei unterschiedliche Hör-/Sehaufträge anzubieten und die Lerngruppe aufzuteilen. Die eine Hälfte beschäftigt sich dann mit Wallis und die andere Hälfte mit dem Konflikt der Brüder. Im Anschluss können die Schüler ihre Ergebnisse vergleichen. Dies könnte in Partnerarbeit mit dem Nachbarn oder auch innerhalb eines Kugellagers (*double circle*), je nach Belieben und vorhandener Zeit, geschehen. Detaillierte Angaben zum Kugellager finden sich in ***Component 5***. Falls die Rahmenbedingungen dies nicht zulassen, können die Aufgaben auch in einem Unterrichtsgespräch gemeinsam besprochen werden.

German DVD
0:54:03–0:58:43

English DVD
0:53:36–0:58:14

Lösungsvorschlag zu *Copy 21:*

A Wallis

1. Wallis calls Elizabeth "the fat Scottish cook".
2. Elizabeth does not greet her, she ignores her and just says hello to the King which offends Wallis, as etiquette means a great deal to her.
   Bertie, on the other hand, is polite and treats Wallis with respect despite her lower status.
3. Wallis feels like the "Queen"/lady of the house. She is the person in charge. She feels very comfortable in high society, as she drinks, smokes, wears clothes that for that time could be considered very sexy and orders the King around.
4. Churchill agrees with Elizabeth's behaviour and thinks that one must greet a member of the Royal family first and not a commoner.
5. The scene reveals Wallis's character and shows that she cannot be accepted as David's wife.

B Bertie and David

1. Bertie wants to talk and complains about the changes at Balmoral. Furthermore, Bertie wants to talk about politics, which is not important to David at all. David neglects his duties according to Bertie. What's more, David intends to marry Wallis and believes Bertie wants to kick him off the throne. Nevertheless, David seems to be more interested in pleasing Wallis than anything else.
2. Bertie starts stammering again and "all the work is down the drain".
3. Different angles are used, first Bertie is portrayed in a low-angle shot, later David is presented in a low-angle shot expressing that he is more powerful than his older brother.
4. This scene is both used to present a step backwards in Bertie's development and to show that the situation with David and Wallis is getting worse so that it will come to a climax later.

4.5 David and Bertie

Im Anschluss an die vorangegangene Szene in Schloss Balmoral ergibt sich erneut die Möglichkeit für eine kreative Aufgabe, bei der sich die Schüler in die Charaktere hineinversetzen müssen. Die Schüler sollen handlungsorientiert mithilfe der Methode *hot seat* zu einem tieferen Filmverständnis gelangen. Detaillierte Angaben zum organisatorischen Vorgehen finden sich unten (*Transparency*). Diese sollte der Lerngruppe in Form einer Folie präsentiert werden, bevor die konkreten Aufgaben (***Copies 19*** und ***20***) vergeben werden.
Mittels dieser *post-viewing activity* können die Schüler ihre erworbenen Kenntnisse über David und Edward anwenden. Die Methode setzt ein hohes Maß an Empathie voraus. Daher sollte nicht die ganze Verantwortung auf einem Schüler lasten, sondern auf mindestens zwei übertragen werden, die sich eine Rolle auf dem *hot seat* (siehe ***Copy 19***) teilen. Ferner sollte kein Schüler gezwungen werden, auf dem *hot seat* Platz zu nehmen. Diese Methode gibt erfahrungsgemäß auch schwächeren Schülern die Möglichkeit, sich in den Unterricht einzubringen, da sie sich zunächst Notizen machen können, bevor es in der Sicherungsphase zur Diskussion kommt (siehe ***Copy 20***). Auch bietet sie sich als Differenzierungsmaßnahme an, da die Schüler, die am Thema besonders interessiert oder in der Lage sind, spontaner und freier zu sprechen, die Rolle auf dem *hot seat* einnehmen können.
In der Diskussionsphase sollte der Lehrer Fehlern gegenüber tolerant sein, diese notieren und in der darauffolgenden Stunde ansprechen, um die Schüler nicht zu verunsichern. Im Vergleich zum Unterrichtsgespräch lässt diese Methode mehr Raum für Kreativität.

Transparency
Hot Seat

Tasks:

Step 1: (5 minutes) Work on your task **alone**:
a) prepare questions and note them down
b) tune into your character and make notes

Step 2: (5 minutes) Discuss your findings with a partner.

Step 3: Show your draft to the teacher
a) your questions
b) your notes

Step 4: Form a half circle with your chairs in the back of the room.
Four chairs have to stand at the front for the people on the *hot seats*.

Step 5: Start asking questions. The people on the *hot seat* try to answer them.

Für viele Schülerinnen und Schüler stellt sich die Frage nach dem Stellenwert der Monarchie in der heutigen Zeit, da diese Regierungsform für sie auf den ersten Blick obsolet erscheint. Eventuell wurde das auch in der Phase der *hot-seat activity* deutlich, da die Argumentation aus Sicht eines Mitglieds der königlichen Familie gegebenenfalls große Abweichungen von der eigenen Meinung und Lebenswirklichkeit verlangt.
Je nach Interessenlage und Informationsstand des Kurses kann im nächsten Schritt ein offenes Unterrichtsgespräch oder eine etwas gelenktere Diskussion nach dem Muster *Think-Pair-Share* zur Frage der Notwendigkeit der Monarchie in der heutigen Zeit angeschlossen

werden. Die Schülerinnen und Schüler können neben ihrer persönlichen Meinung auch auf Vorwissen aus ***Component 2*** zu den Aufgaben und Pflichten von Monarchen zurückgreifen. Falls die Diskussion an dieser Stelle noch nicht geführt werden soll, kann die Fragestellung auch im Zusammenhang mit den *post-viewing activities* und unterstützt durch weitere Materialien in ***Component 6.5*** behandelt werden.

Do we need a Royal Family?

1. **Think:** Work on your own. Write down pros and cons in a grid.
2. **Pair:** Work with a partner and compare your notes.
3. **Share:** Meet with another pair. Two must be in favour of the Royal Family and two would like to abolish the monarchy. Discuss the question. Come to a well-founded decision.

Mögliche Argumente:

PROS:

- head of state who is above party politics
- has the best interests of nation at heart rather than other considerations, e.g. party interests
- represents centuries of history and tradition
- regarded as archaic by some but brings in lots of money as tourists are interested in seeing palaces/buying souvenirs etc.
- important element of continuity within a democratic system
- Monarchy can lead public opinion. Although above party politics, modern monarchs have proved capable of raising important and sometimes unpopular issues that otherwise would have been ignored. For example, in the U.K. Prince Charles has legitimised discussion of environmental issues and stimulated a lively debate about the purpose of architecture, while Princess Diana's work with Aids sufferers helped shift public opinion.
- links with other states

CONS:

- head of state not elected by the people
- hereditary head of state does not necessarily denote intelligence, as likely to get complete idiot as well as well-read, intelligent monarch
- monarch represents class system not equality
- costs are unjustifiable: luxurious lifestyle paid by taxes
- members of the Royal Family have at times become national embarrassment instead of people one could be proud of: Charles and Camilla
- religiously discriminatory; British society is multi-faith; thus an Anglican head of state is no longer needed
- monarchy makes UK look backwards

The King's Speech – Bertie and his father

German DVD
0:28:23–0:31:48

English DVD
0:27:55–0:31:19

1. Describe King George V and his relationship to his son Bertie.

2. Note down striking cinematic devices that are used to underline the relationship.

3. Sum up how the role of a king has changed according to George V.

4. State the problems the British Empire faces according to George V.

5. Note down the function(s) of the scene.

6. King George V wrote a letter to his son Bertie on the occasion of his 5th birthday:

Now that you are five years old I hope you will always try to be obedient, do at once what you are told, as you will find it will come much easier to you the sooner you begin. I always tried to do this when I was your age & found it made me much happier.

Analyse to what extent this letter reflects the father-son relationship shown in the film.

Her Majesty Queen Elizabeth II

[...] At the age of 12, having already distinguished herself as a gifted and eager horsewoman, Princess Elizabeth confided to her teacher that, had she not been born to be Queen, she would "like to be a lady living in the country with lots of horses and dogs". [...] Princess Elizabeth was initially educated at home, although the Duchess of York had always harboured the hope that one day her daughter would attend public school, and thus learn about matters both intellectual and social. This, however, was not to be, as the new King, Edward VIII, had decided that it would not do for a Princess to be educated alongside commoners, and thus Elizabeth received the entirety of her instruction in private.

Given contemporary circumstances, it may well have been the case that the King was merely trying to minimise the level of press scrutiny on the affairs of the Royal Family. His relationship with Wallis Simpson was soon to become the United Kingdom's most popular source of common gossip, and there can be little doubt that he was apprehensive as to the public reaction when news of her divorce came to light. By the end of 1937, Elizabeth's life had changed dramatically: Edward VIII had abdicated, her father had been crowned King George VI, and she was Heiress Presumptive to the Throne.

Despite the requisite move to Buckingham Palace, and the ever-increasing pressure of life as the daughter of the King, the 11-year-old Elizabeth was essentially unchanged. Her propensity for pranks and play had been replaced by a more mature and responsible attitude to life and duty, but her formidable sense of humour remained very much intact.

As befitted an Heiress Presumptive, she took it upon herself to discover all she could about the matters that would one day form the basis of her ruling life. She began to attend lessons in constitutional history at Eton College, one of England's most illustrious and intellectually demanding public schools. Soon, her love of all things historical led her to broaden her education in order to take in the history of Europe. A famous anecdote recounts the occasion on which Princess Marie Louise apologised to her fellow guests at a dinner party held at Windsor Castle for having spoken for so long about her life. With her customary warmth and sincerity, Princess Elizabeth answered: "But Cousin Louise, it's history, and therefore so thrilling!"

[When war came in September 1939] Princess Elizabeth decided it was time to show that she was ready to assume the full weight of her Royal responsibilities. Realising the need to boost morale, she became patron of organisations whose work she valued. Already President of charities such as the Queen Elizabeth Hospital for Children in Hackney, east London, and the National Society for the Prevention of Cruelty to Children, she embarked on a series of national visits with the King and Queen. She first bore the full weight of regal office at the age of 18, in 1944, when, during the King's absence on a tour of the Italian battlefields, she performed many of the official duties of Head of State.

[...] The Princess's role in service had demonstrated that "Lilibet" was now a mature and natural leader. Furthermore, she had achieved her majority. It was with little surprise, but much joy, that the public was informed of her engagement to Lieutenant Philip Mountbatten, son of Prince Andrew of Greece and great-great-grandson of Queen Victoria. The couple had known each other for many years, and thus Prince Philip was the obvious and most popular match for Elizabeth, in the eyes of both senior courtiers and the British public. Even the characteristically fickle British press conceded that this was "clearly a match of choice not arrangement".

But as a new generation of the Royal Family was born, another began to fade. By 1952, King George VI was so seriously ill that Princess Elizabeth and her husband stepped in to take his place on a State visit to Australia and New Zealand. On their way there, in Kenya, the Heiress Presumptive was brought the news that her beloved father was dead, and that she had acceded to the Throne. On June 2, 1953, as news of the Commonwealth's conquest of Mount Everest arrived, the Princess returned to Westminster Abbey, in which she had been married just a few years earlier, to be crowned "Elizabeth the Second, by the Grace of God, of the United Kingdom of Great Britain and Northern Ireland and Her other Realms and Territories Queen, Head of the Commonwealth, Defender of the Faith".

Princess Elizabeth had become Queen Elizabeth II, but she had never quite ceased to be "Lilibet" – the little girl who knew both her duty and her own mind, and was determined to be the best and the most "normal" regent that she could.

Source: http://www.britainexpress.com/royals/queen.htm [6 12 2012]

Hot Seat

David

Tune into your character. Step into David's shoes. This will help you to play his role in the hot seat better. Here are some ideas to help you. Take notes – remember that the ideas have to be based on the film. If the information is not in the story, you will have to guess.

What is your relationship to the members of your family like?

What is your greatest strength?

What is your greatest weakness?

What are you afraid of?

What is important for you?

What is your biggest problem at the moment?

How do you feel with regard to your duties?

How do you imagine your future life? ...

COPY 19

Hot Seat

Bertie

Tune into your character. Step into Bertie's shoes. This will help you to play his role in the hot seat better. Here are some ideas to help you. Take notes – remember that the ideas have to be based on the film. If the information is not in the story, you will have to guess.

What is your relationship to the members of your family like, especially to your elder brother?

What is your greatest strength?

What is your greatest weakness?

What are you afraid of?

What is important for you?

What is your biggest problem at the moment?

How do you feel with regard to your duties?

How do you imagine your future life?

How much does your wife mean to you? ....

Hot Seat

Your job is to think of questions which can be put to David/Edward VIII. What would you like to ask him if you met him?

You can ask him…

- about his situation
- his feelings
- his fears
- his problems
- his relationships to both Wallis and his brother
- his past
- his future
- his mistakes
- etc.

For example:
How did you feel when Bertie reminded you of your duties at Balmoral Castle?

Hot Seat

Your job is to think of questions to Bertie. What would you like to ask him if you met him?

You can ask him…

- about his situation
- his feelings
- his fears
- his problems
- his relationship to his brother
- his childhood
- his future
- his mistakes
- etc.

For example:
How did you feel when Lionel suggested you should put David off the throne?

The King's Speech – Wallis Simpson and Bertie and David

Tasks for A

1. Note down what Wallis Simpson calls Elizabeth.
2. Sum up how Elizabeth and Bertie treat Wallis and think of possible reasons for Elizabeth's behaviour.
3. Note down your impression of Wallis Simpson.
4. Note down what Churchill thinks about Elizabeth's behaviour.
5. Note down the function of the scene.

Tasks for B

1. Describe the conflict between Bertie and David.
2. What consequence does this conflict have for Bertie?
3. Note down striking cinematic devices.
4. Note down the function of the scene.

Component 5

A strange friendship

In diesem *Component* geht es um die Beschäftigung mit den eigenartigen Beziehungen in *The King's Speech*. Hier steht die Freundschaft zwischen Lionel und Bertie im Mittelpunkt, da der *Duke of York* laut der filmischen Darstellung nie Freunde hatte und erst durch Lionel erfährt, was es bedeutet, einen wahren Freund zu haben. Darüber hinaus bietet der *Component* aber auch die Möglichkeit, sich mit der Beziehung von Wallis und Edward auseinanderzusetzen, da dieses ungleiche Paar auch noch heute die Medien fasziniert und Stoff für zahlreiche Spielfilme, Artikel und Bücher bietet. Anschließend wird in diesem *Component* die Beziehung von Wallis und Edward VIII zu Hitler angesprochen, die neben der Abdankung einen weiteren Kritikpunkt an der Person Davids darstellt.
Zur Vorbereitung auf die Klausur dienen die Probeklausur mit dem Text von Shasta Nelson und einem Filmausschnitt (***Copy 22***) sowie die *Tool Box "How to write a letter"*. Ferner werden *Mediation*, Gedichtanalyse und Textarbeit in diesem *Component* trainiert. Zuletzt ergibt sich die Möglichkeit, den Film auf seinen Wahrheitsgehalt zu überprüfen. Hierzu ermöglicht ***Copy 26*** den Einblick in einen Brief von *Queen Elizabeth, The Queen Mother* zu erhalten. Ein weiterer Artikel (***Copy 27***) beschäftigt sich ferner mit der Frage, wie viel Wahrheit sich in *The King's Speech* verbirgt. **Copy 27** ist leicht verständlich und als Arbeitsblatt oder Hausaufgabe einsetzbar.

5.1 Bertie and Lionel

Im Rahmen der Probeklausur (***Copy 22***) wird zunächst der ausgewählte Filmausschnitt zweimal gezeigt, zu dem die Schüler Notizen anfertigen sollen. Wichtig ist hier, dass den Schülerinnen und Schülern zuvor ausreichend Zeit gegeben wird, damit sie sich mit der Aufgabenstellung der Klausur vertraut machen können. Danach erhalten sie etwa 40 Minuten Zeit, den Klausurtext zu bearbeiten. Anschließend kann die Filmszene evtl. ein weiteres Mal präsentiert werden. Bei Aufgabe 3 dürfen die Schüler wie in einer realen Testsituation zwischen einer kreativen Aufgabe und einer Meinungsäußerung wählen. Falls das Verfassen eines Briefes noch nicht geübt wurde, bietet die *Tool Box "How to write a personal letter"* weiter unten Hilfestellung, da dieses Textformat in beiden Klausurvorschlägen auch gefordert wird.

German DVD
1:00:10–1:02:34
English DVD
0:58:15–1:02:06

Es wurde eine Szene gewählt, in der es zu einem Bruch in der Freundschaft zwischen Lionel und Bertie kommt. Der Text von Shasta Nelson zielt darauf ab, wie schwer es für hochrangige Personen ist, echte Freunde zu finden. Auf dieser Grundlage wird zum einen Berties Problematik deutlich und zum anderen kann am Ende eine Diskussion geführt werden, ob die Beziehung zwischen den beiden als wahre Freundschaft bezeichnet werden kann.

How to write a personal letter

There are no fixed rules for personal letters as they are individual. Nevertheless, there are some components every letter has:

1. **The Greeting** Start your letter with "Dear".
2. **The Introduction** Begin the body of your letter with a reference to a previous letter or an opening question, like "How are you?".
3. **The Body** State why you're writing. Organize your main part into paragraphs. Skip a line when you introduce a new thought.
4. **The Conclusion** This shows that the letter is going to end, e.g. "Hope to hear from you soon."
5. **Final Words** Close your letter with "Best wishes", "Love" or "Yours".

Don't forget that the closer the relationship between the writer and the addressee is, the less formal your letter can be; this means that the use of colloquial language and short forms is allowed.

Lösungsvorschlag zu *Copy 22*:

1. It's lonely at the top, because …
- people are looked up to, but not seen (ll. 16f.)
- there are no real friends; people are used by others to make themselves feel more important or friendship is used for personal gains (ll. 20f.)
- important people feel too important to deal with lower people (ll. 29ff.)
- people put others on a pedestal (l. 31)

2.
- they talk about Bertie's problems like friends
- equals
- handheld camera in the park makes the scene more dramatic
- when thy talk about Wallis it is foggy first, but there is a light, calm atmosphere
- face to face as if they are alone, stressed through fog
- quiet atmosphere
- when Lionel touches Bertie he starts screaming and gets angry; the movement stops
- medium shots are used to show the feelings of the two men

3. a) Lösungsvorschlag/mögliches Tafelbild:

business relationship	**friendship**
first Bertie is sceptical	Lionel always treats him like an equal and is very patient
Bertie doesn't want to talk about his childhood to him; doesn't feel the need to open up	after King George's death they get closer, Bertie opens up and finally talks about his childhood; Lionel is a good listener
Bertie won't listen to Lionel's opinion	Lionel behaves like a real friend and tells him his honest opinion and that he thinks Bertie would be a good king
in the park they are not presented as equal; when Bertie is being touched, he realizes that he is superior and starts screaming	at the beginning of the scene there's an equal relationship in the therapy room and in the first minutes of their walk

➡ all in all, one can say that Lionel has always been Bertie's friend as he has always been patient, understanding, critical and honest
Bertie, on the other hand, needed some time to open up and to understand that friends must be allowed to say what they are thinking; that's why Bertie apologizes in the end

b) individual solutions

5.2 Wallis and Edward

Abgesehen von der ungewöhnlichen Freundschaft zwischen Albert und Lionel ist gewiss auch die Beziehung zwischen David/Edward und Wallis nicht nur für damalige, sondern auch noch für heutige Verhältnisse erstaunlich. Der Thronfolger, der eine geschiedene (und anfangs sogar noch in zweiter Ehe verheiratete) Frau liebt, diese Beziehung gegen alle Widerstände aufrecht erhält und schließlich sogar seinen Thron dafür opfert, hat die „abdication crisis" nach nur elf Monaten seiner Regentschaft ausgelöst.
Wallis Simpson begegnet den Zuschauern im Film zum ersten Mal während der Party auf Balmoral. Ausgehend davon werden die folgenden Texte behandelt. Um den Schülerinnen und Schülern ein tieferes Verständnis der eigenwilligen Beziehung von Edward und Wallis und den unvermeidlichen Folgen zu ermöglichen, wurden ein Gedicht und zwei Zeitungsartikel als Hintergrundinformationen gewählt.
Neben zahlreichen anderen hat sich auch der irische Dichter William Butler Yeats (1865–1939) in einem seiner Gedichte mit dieser grundlegenden Entscheidung beschäftigt und kommt dabei zu dem Schluss, dass nicht der Thron, sondern das persönliche Glück in einer zwischenmenschlichen Beziehung das weitaus höhere Gut ist (*Copy 23*).

Lösungsvorschlag zu *Copy 23*:

1. This poem deflates politics and shows them to depend exclusively on love. The first two stanzas reveal the arrogance and lofty attitude of ruling people in general, but the third stanza takes up the topic of King Edward VIII and his abdication because of his wish to marry Wallis Simpson.
2. Yeats wants to praise Edward VIII with his poem for giving up his throne for love. The poem consists of three stanzas of equal length, each ending in the

question if a man should keep his lover waiting. This regular pattern is also kept in the rhyme scheme.
Yeats's ambivalence about politics in general is shown here. "Those cheers that can be bought or sold" show the monarch's lack of care for the people as he, on his "modern throne", is corrupt and weak ("That office fools have run"). The "waxen seal" and "that signature" express that there is not much to the position of a king or queen but meaningless symbols or procedures. Yeats then comes to the question "what decent man would keep his lover waiting" for this office so devoid of meaning and importance and implicitely draws the conclusion that Edward VIII did the only right thing when listening to his heart and turning his back on his duties.

3. individual answers

Der weiterführende Text (***Copy 24***) liefert Hintergrundinformationen sowohl zur Biografie Wallis Simpsons als auch zur Einstellung der Öffentlichkeit ihr gegenüber. Er eignet sich besonders wegen seiner Länge und Schwierigkeit eher als Zusatztext für einen Leistungskurs. Als Einsatzmöglichkeit bietet sich die Verlagerung des Textes als Hausaufgabe oder als arbeitsteilige Partnerarbeit im Unterricht an. Hierzu ist die Methode *double circle* (Kugellager) angedacht. Hierbei erarbeiten sich die Schüler den Text arbeitsteilig eigenständig (lesen und Notizen), stellen sich anschließend in zwei Doppelkreisen einander gegenüber auf und berichten sich gegenseitig über ihre Stichpunkte. Nach einigen Minuten bewegt sich der Außenkreis drei Personen weiter und die sich nun gegenüber stehenden Schüler berichten einander über ihr Thema. Die Übung kann je nach Lerngruppe mehrere Durchgänge lang wiederholt werden.

Lösungsvorschlag zu *Copy 24*:

1: Wallis's life	2: public opinion
born in Baltimore in 1896 (l. 31)	did the nation an enormous service when she made it impossible for Edward VIII to stay King (ll. 3f.).
father died when she was young, mother had a boarding house (ll. 32–34)	nobody of substance would stay close to them (l. 18)
married Lieutenant Winfield Spencer Jnr in 1916 (l. 37)	George VI denied her the title HRH (l. 19)
divorced him as he was aggressive; Wallis led an independent life in Shanghai where she learned some tricks from prostitutes (ll. 39ff.)	prostitute, Yankee harlot, sadistic, cold, overbearing, vain, lowest of the low (ll. 23ff.)
married Ernest Simpson in 1928 (l. 46)	Royal Family was "filled with icy menace" towards her (l. 27)
learned British etiquette from Barbara Cartland (l. 47)	different behaviour from normal court protocol (ll. 28f.)
lived for parties, that is where she met David (ll. 49f.)	impossible as the partner of the heir to the throne (ll. 63f.)
abdication crisis in 1936 (ll. 62f.)	
exile in the Bahamas (l. 15) and in Paris (l. 66)	

Eine weiterführende Diskussion über den Text kann angeschlossen werden:

> Would Wallis and Edward have the same problems today?
>
> Do you agree with Sebba's and Lewis's opinion that "Wallis saved us all from a fascist Britain"?

Die erste Frage wird den Schülerinnen und Schülern die heutige *Royal Family* in Erinnerung rufen und damit das Beispiel von Camilla und Prince Charles, der ebenso wie Edward zu Beginn des Films direkter Thronfolger ist. Prince Charles ist hingegen nicht nur selbst geschieden, sondern hat auch eine bereits geschiedene Frau in zweiter Ehe geheiratet, sodass die Problematik für Wallis und Edward sich heute offensichtlich nicht so ergeben würde.
Hinsichtlich der zweiten Frage kann man dem Autor zustimmen, dass Wallis – wenngleich unabsichtlich und indirekt – einen großen Einfluss auf die politischen Entwicklungen in Großbritannien hatte.

5.3 Edward, Wallis and Hitler

Um die umstrittene Rolle von Edward VIII und Wallis Simpson während der verschiedenen politischen Strömungen vor dem Zweiten Weltkrieg zu beleuchten, enthüllt der deutsche Spiegel-Text in ***Copy 25 b*** Hintergründe zu im Film nicht erwähnten zweifelhaften Haltungen. Als Mediationsübung sollen hier die wesentlichen Aussagen ins Englische übertragen werden. Entweder als Einstieg oder als Alternative bietet sich der Einsatz des Bildes (***Copy 25 a***) an. Zunächst sollen die Schülerinnen und Schüler das Bild beschreiben und Vermutungen anstellen, wie Edward zu Hitler steht. Aufgrund der Körpersprache und des Gesichtsausdrucks liegt der Verdacht einer freundschaftlichen Beziehung zwischen Hitler und Edward nahe.

Lösungsvorschlag zu *Copy 25 a*:

- Wallis Simpson and Hitler shaking hands, Edward next to Wallis
- smiling faces, obviously relaxed atmosphere
- no apparent differences
- hint of deference on the part of Edward?

Lösungsvorschlag zu *Copy 25 b*:

Wallis and Edward thought they could spend a relaxed time in Florida in April 1941 but US President Roosevelt had ordered a secret surveillance operation. A 227-page long FBI report shows that both the Duke and the Duchess of Windsor had sympathies for Hitler and his Nazi regime. If Hitler had won, Edward VIII would have been Hitler's puppet king. This is also proved by new documents such as Sir Alan Lascelles's diary (he was secretary to the Duke).
All these new documents show that Edward would have conspired with Hitler and that Wallis Simpson played a major role, having had intimate relations with Nazi representatives. Edward's abdication can be seen in a new light now.

5.4 Truth & Fiction

Die Materialien zu Wallis Simpson führen bereits von der filmimmanenten Analyse weiter zu einer Betrachtung des historischen Kontexts, die – zum Beispiel in einer Hausaufgabe – weitergeführt werden kann. Es bietet sich an, anhand von ausgewählten Texten den Wahrheitsgehalt einiger Aspekte des Filmes zu überprüfen. Hier sollte zunächst als Einstieg ein Brief von *Queen Elizabeth* (*The Queen Mother*) erwähnt werden (***Copy 26***), in welchem sie sich bei Lionel Logue bedankt.

Lösungsvorschlag zu *Copy 26*:

Queen Elizabeth The Queen Mother thinks Lionel helped Bertie very much both with his speech impediment and his entire view of life. That is why she would always be grateful to him.

Die kritische Auseinandersetzung mit dem historischen Wahrheitsgehalt des ganzen Filmes auf der Grundlage einer Filmrezension von David Freeman, der an der *California State University Fullerton* Geschichte unterrichtet, erfolgt im Anschluss (***Copy 27***).

Where does Freeman identify artistic licence and what does he point out to be historically correct? How does he judge the changes Seidler made?

Lösungsvorschlag zu *Copy 27*:

events and facts that have been changed

- the film mentions neither Churchill's support for Edward VIII nor George VI's support for Chamberlain's appeasement of the Nazis
- Bertie's first speech has been advanced from 1925 to shortly before 1936
- Bertie went to see Logue as early as 1926
- there were no misunderstandings between the two men at the beginning: Seidler used "informed imagination" to create the film's therapy scenes, he projected his own experience into the creation of the film character Logue
- according to Logue's grandchildren Logue never used Christian names when adressing the King
- there was never any question about Logue being a doctor; Bertie always referred to him as "Mr. Logue" or "Logue"
- very fast, the treatment was extremely successful, which made George V so delighted that Bertie became his favourite son
- Bertie chose his name George out of respect for his father and not because Churchill suggested that Albert sounded "too German"

historically correct events and facts

- beside the general story and the characters, who are all historical figures, all biographies of George VI mention his relationship with Logue
- Seidler could include insights from Logue's notebooks

general judgement

- some changes are understandable, but require further adaptations to make the story believable
- artistic licence gives the film more dramatic interest
- historians must be true to the facts, but dramatists need to tell a story

Eine tiefer gehende Bearbeitung der Frage nach „truth or fiction" mit kritischeren Quellen ist z. B. möglich durch den Text „Churchill Didn't Say That. The King's Speech is riddled with gross falsifications of history." von Christopher Hitchens, der aufgrund seiner Komplexität eine Möglichkeit der Binnendifferenzierung für sehr gute Schülerinnen und Schüler bietet. (http://www.slate.com/articles/news_and_politics/fighting_words/2011/01/churchill_didnt_say_that.single.html [12.07.2012]). Für weitere Studien empfehlen sich in der Bibliografie aufgeführte Werke (u. a. die Biografie von George VI von Sarah Bradford, siehe S. 14).

The King's Speech – Mock Exam

Text: Shasta Nelson: "There's a reason it's lonely at the top", 4 March 2011

Film scene: German DVD 1:00:10-1:02:34/English DVD 0:58:15-01:02:06

We often assume that loneliness or a sense of social disconnection is for those people [at the top]. We picture some angry, hurt, unfriendly, socially awkward and un-lovable woman sitting in a dark house, with the curtains closed, alone. Maybe a dozen cats. (...) One of the most poignant lines in the Oscar-winning movie, The King's Speech, came from Colin Firth, playing King George VI, when he muttered "I wouldn't know" in response to his speech therapists nonchalant statement „That's what friends are for." As king, everyone is forced to be friendly and adoring and respectful to him, but that doesn't mean he feels known, supported, liked or seen for who he is beyond his title.

On an obviously much smaller scale, many of us know what it feels like to be looked up to, but not seen. Some of it is the fault of those who simply want to be near the popular and powerful for what it does for them: making them feel more important, giving them greater access and using the friendship to their own gains.

But some of it is also the fault of those who are the adored. The desire to reveal the best image, to stay liked, to be a role model puts an inane amount of pressure to not really share honestly, be seen with our faults, or risk getting hurt.

There's a reason they say it's lonely at the top. Whether the person at the top starts to feel too amazing to connect with those beneath them, or those beneath them begin to treat the top as though they are on a pedestal; a painful dynamic seems to isolate those who excel in other areas. In my work as a life coach and pastor, I have seen first-hand the loneliness of those who are too beautiful, too talented, too powerful, too famous and too wealthy.

(...) In the movie The King's Speech, Lionel Logue, the speech therapist played by Geoffrey Rush, lacked credentials, fame, a posh office, success in his own acting ambitions and a home that was sufficient for hosting royalty. What he had was the ability to both believe more in the King than the King did himself, while also creating an equal relationship, insisting on calling him Bertie and setting ground rules that he chose.

Rush's character held his own, believing in his own worth and what he could offer (even in the midst of vast inequality). He also never lost sight of how human the King really was, seeing him with his imperfections and wounds. He saw him – his amazingness and his insecurities.

Isn't that what we all crave?

And the final line of The King's Speech came onto a black screen before the credits rolled, attesting that it can work: "Bertie and Lionel remained friends throughout their entire life."

http://www.psychologytoday.com/print/56513

1. Outline the reasons Shasta Nelson mentions as to why "it's lonely at the top". (comprehension)
2. Analyse Bertie's relationship with Lionel Logue and the impact it had on Bertie. Pay special attention to the given scene and the cinematic devices that support the atmosphere. (analysis)
3. Choose between the following two tasks:
   a) Comment on Bertie's and Lionel's relationship in the film. Are they real friends or is Lionel just another person who uses Bertie to become more popular? Discuss the question and give examples from the whole film. (comment)

   or

   b) Imagine you are Lionel. Write a letter to Bertie in which you explain yourself and apologize for your behaviour in the park. (re-creation of text)

William Butler Yeats: A Model For The Laureate (1937)

On thrones from China to Peru
All sorts of kings have sat
That men and women of all sorts
proclaimed both good and great;
And what's the odds if such as these
For reason of the State
Should keep their lovers waiting,
Keep their lovers waiting?

Some boast of beggar-kings and kings
Of rascals black and white
That rule because a strong right arm
Puts all men in a fright,
And drunk or sober live at ease
Where none gainsay their right,
And keep their lovers waiting,
Keep their lovers waiting.

The Muse is mute when public men
Applaud a modern throne:
Those cheers that can be bought or sold,
That office fools have run,
That waxen seal, that signature.
For things like these what decent man
Would keep his lover waiting,
Keep his lover waiting?

William Butler Yeats: New poems. Dublin, Ire., The Cuala press, 1938.

1. Sum up what the poem is about.
2. Analyse the poem.
3. Comment on Yeat's question: "[W]hat decent man would keep his lover waiting?"

Roger Lewis: "That Woman: The Life of Wallis Simpson, Duchess of Windsor by Anne Sebba", 2 September 2011

That Woman by Anne Sebba, a new biography of Wallis Simpson, rescues her from the vilification she endured in her own lifetime, says Roger Lewis.

vilification *Verleumdung, Verunglimpfung*

Should Wallis Simpson be awarded a posthumous George Cross? It becomes abundantly clear in Anne Sebba's biography that the late Duchess of Windsor did Britain an enormous service when she allowed Edward VIII to abdicate so he could run off with her.

The Prince of Wales was more than a liability – he was "a depressed adolescent... worryingly unsafe, he could be certified", according to Lord Wigram, George V's private secretary. "Certain cells in his brain have never grown," murmured another courtier, Sir Alan Lascelles.

liability *Belastung*

courtier *Höfling*

Madness was less of a problem, though, than the Prince's chumminess with the Germans and pro-appeasement politicians. He and Wallis were feted by Mussolini in Venice, stayed at the Ritz in Madrid when Spain was run by Franco and visited Hitler in Berchtesgaden, where they were photographed among the swastikas. The Nazis "were ready to exploit the King's sympathies", and even after the abdication there were plans to install him as a puppet monarch should Britain have been successfully invaded.

chumminess *Freundschaft, Geselligkeit*

By August 1940, however, the government had exiled the Windsors to the Bahamas, "the Empire's most backward-looking colony". The remainder of their lives was to be spent in an aimless, boring round of luncheons with dressmakers and dinners with jewellers. Nobody of substance would venture near them – and George VI was adamant that Wallis should never be referred to as HRH as it would be "a great mistake to acknowledge Mrs Simpson as a suitable person to become Royal".

adamant *unnachgiebig*

This was spiteful. While we can all agree that the ex-King was a petulant pipsqueak, who would have made a disastrous monarch, it does seem that everyone took it out on Wallis. She was generally vilified as a "prostitute, a Yankee harlot", "sadistic, cold, overbearing, vain", "mean and grasping" and, in the words of the late Queen Elizabeth, "the lowest of the low".

petulant *launisch*
pipsqueak *unbedeutendes Würstchen*

Well prior to the Prince of Wales commencing his open pursuit of her, Wallis was correct to surmise that the Royal family was "filled with an icy menace for such as me". Part of Wallis's appeal, clearly, was that she represented the very polar opposite of the stifling Victorian court protocol. She implied freedom. But as Anne Sebba shows, Wallis was cramped by her own "mounting nervous tensions".

to surmise *vermuten*

stifling *beengend*

Born in Baltimore in 1896, Wallis's father was "a charmingly sensitive but melancholy consumptive", who died almost immediately after his daughter's birth, and her mother, suddenly in straitened circumstances, ran a residential hotel – which meant the family were "branded as boarding-house keepers". Wallis, for the remainder of her life, was "paralysed by fear" at the thought of being reduced again to such shabby-genteel conditions.

consumptive *Schwindsüchtiger*

In 1916 she married Lieutenant Winfield Spencer Jnr, who turned out to be a violent alcoholic. Wallis had been "blind to the bitter streak in him", but it was a streak soon enough discovered by each of his four wives, who divorced him for his "irritability and irascibility, cruelty and abusive behaviour".

irascibility *Jähzorn*

Wallis then went to live an independent life in Shanghai, where, if Sebba is to be believed, "she learnt from Chinese prostitutes some ancient oriental techniques for pleasuring men" and "appeared in naughty postcards". Poor old Ernest Simpson probably didn't know what hit him when he invited her "to make up a fourth at bridge".

Simpson, the grandson of Polish Jews, owned a shipping firm and had "an air of security and breeding" that Wallis craved. They were married in 1928 and Barbara Cartland taught Wallis "the niceties of British etiquette".

Barbara Cartland *(1901–2000) war eine englische Autorin und selbst ernannte Expertin für Romantik*

It was parties that Wallis rather lived for – and she used up her docile husband's resources on couture clothes and giving lavish dinners. The Prince of Wales was soon a grateful guest. As soon as he saw her, he was besotted. Wallis, too, was susceptible, as, with Simpson out at the office, her days, she admitted, "stretched vacantly before me". The more Wallis dared to "taunt and berate" the Prince in public, the more he relished it. No one had dared treat him like that before. The Simpsons were soon bidden to Fort Belvedere on a weekly basis. "I think I do amuse him," Wallis told her family in Baltimore. "I'm the comedy relief and we like to dance together but I always have Ernest hanging around my neck so all is safe."

But not for long. The Prince decided he wanted Wallis as his bride, no matter the consequences. Wallis herself was terrified, as what would happen if Simpson divorced her and the capricious Prince dropped her? She'd have nothing. In any event, says Sebba, Wallis was never in love with the Prince, only with "the opulence, the lifestyle" that he was providing.

Consternation ensued. The press, government, church, the dominions' prime ministers, even probably the fire brigade, couldn't conceive of "the idea of a woman with two living husbands consorting with the heir to the throne". If Wallis felt "every inch the hunted animal", and if "every day from now on was lived in the shadow of 1936", then it was a rather pampered "hellish exile" – with a mansion in Paris, liveried servants, a tax-free allowance and offshore investments siphoned off from the Duchy of Cornwall estates. The Windsors were always buying each other trinkets from Cartier, which were auctioned after their deaths for $50,281,887. But better that desiccated and indulgent existence than the alternative – the prospect of a sieg heiling monarch on the balcony of Buckingham Palace. By staying with him, Wallis saved us all from a fascist Britain.

lavish *verschwenderisch*
besotted *vernarrt*
to taunt *spotten*
to berate *beschimpfen*
trinkets *kleine Schmuckstücke*
desiccated *vertrocknet*
indulgent *genussvoll*

1. Make notes on Wallis Simpson's life.
2. Summarise public opinion of Wallis.

COPY 25 a

Duke and Duchess of Windsor meet Adolf Hitler (1937)

Describe the persons in the photo. What can you say about the atmosphere?

COPY 25 b

Ein König und die Nazis

Als der Herzog und die Herzogin von Windsor im April 1941 in Florida anlegten, glaubten sie, sie könnten mitten während des Zweiten Weltkriegs ein paar entspannte Tage an Amerikas Sonnenküste verbringen.

Aber: Am Vorabend hatte US-Präsident Theodore Roosevelt persönlich eine außerordentliche Geheimdienstoperation angeordnet. Die Überwachungsprotokolle wurden erst kürzlich der Öffentlichkeit zugänglich.

Auf 227 Seiten zeichnet dieser FBI-Report über den abgedankten britischen König Edward VIII. ein unglaubliches Bild. Der Herzog und die Herzogin von Windsor haben kaum verhüllt Nazi-Sympathien gehegt und mit Adolf Hitlers Drittem Reich konspiriert.

Der Vorfahre von Königin Elizabeth II. war als Marionettenkönig vorgesehen, hätte Hitler England besiegt. Neben dem FBI-Report sind zahlreiche neue Dokumente aufgetaucht, etwa das private Tagebuch von Sir Alan Lascelles, dem Privatsekretär des Herzogs.

Alle neuen Dokumente gemeinsam beweisen, dass der frühere englische König tatsächlich zum Verrat an seiner Heimat bereit war und seine Sympathien bei Adolf Hitler und dem Nazireich lagen. Die Rolle seiner Ehefrau Wallis Simpson, einer amerikanischen Staatsbürgerin, wird überaus deutlich. Sie hatte eigene – auch intime Beziehungen – zu hohen Vertretern des NS-Regimes. Die Abdankung von Edward VIII. erscheint durch die jetzt freigegebenen Dokumente in einem neuen historischen Licht.

SPIEGEL ONLINE
http://www.spiegel.de/sptv/geschichte/a-798561.html [14 02 2013]

Imagine you get this text in the history lesson and the exchange student in your class needs your help. Outline the contents of the text for him.

Queen Elizabeth's posthumous endorsement of Lionel Logue

Tim Walker: The King's Speech hero is thanked by the late Queen Elizabeth the Queen Mother in a touching newly-discovered letter, 6 December 2010

The Queen Mother told Lionel Logue that her husband had owed him a debt of gratitude for helping him not merely with his stutter, but his whole life

With the forthcoming film *The King's Speech* already prompting a debate about the extent to which Lionel Logue, George VI's speech therapist, really did help the wartime monarch, a posthumous endorsement has come from the late Queen Elizabeth, the Queen Mother.

In a newly-discovered handwritten letter on Buckingham Palace notepaper, dated February 28, 1952, Queen Elizabeth told Logue that her husband had owed him a debt of gratitude for helping him not merely with his stutter, but his whole life.

"I think that I know perhaps better than anyone just how much you helped the King, not only with his speech, but, through that, his whole life, and outlook on life," she wrote to Logue one year before his death. "I shall always be deeply grateful to you for all you did for him." Of the King, she added: "He was such a splendid person, and I don't believe that he ever thought of himself at all. I did so hope that he might have been allowed a few years of comparative peace after the many anguished years he had to battle through so bravely. But it was not to be." Queen Elizabeth's letter to Logue was unearthed by the Australian speech therapist's grandson, Mark, among family papers a few months ago.

Its contents are not included in the film *The King's Speech* which opens in the New Year and stars Colin Firth as George VI, Helena Bonham Carter as Queen Elizabeth and Geoffrey Rush as Lionel Logue.

They are, however, included in a book of the same name by Mark Logue and Peter Conradi which is published this week. "Like so many of his generation, my grandfather never boasted of his achievements," Logue told me. "It's only now, after writing my book, that I feel I know him."

Sum up how far Lionel Logue helped Bertie according to Queen Elizabeth, the Queen Mother.

David Freeman: "Perspective: How true is 'The King's Speech'?", 13 February 2011

Screenwriter David Seidler did some tweaking and telescoping to tell his tale, a history professor writes, but it was done to advance the story, plus explore the relationship between the stuttering royal and his commoner therapist.

If any best-picture contender was going to face questions about taking liberties with the facts this Oscar season, it seemed likely it would be "The Social Network." But now that screenwriter Aaron Sorkin and Facebook founder Mark Zuckerberg have tactfully retreated a bit from their initially contentious stands, the accuracy debate has shifted to "The King's Speech."

"The King's Speech" is being sold as a feel-good tale of how a friendship between a royal and a commoner affected the course of history. But some commentators are complaining, among other things, that the film covers up Winston Churchill's support for Edward VIII, the playboy king who abdicated to marry an American divorcee, and that the movie fails to acknowledge that the once tongue-tied George VI supported Prime Minister Neville Chamberlain's appeasement of the Nazis. (Writing last month at slate.com, Christopher Hitchens blasted the film as "a gross falsification of history.")

As a specialist in British history, I agree that screenwriter David Seidler certainly has tweaked the record a bit and telescoped events in "The King's Speech" – but for the same artistic reasons that have guided writers from Shakespeare to Alan Bennett, who wrote the screenplay for "The Madness of King George" (and the play on which the movie was based). While historians must stick to the facts, dramatists need to tell a good story in good time. It also helps if they can explore the human condition in the process.

Seidler's script opens with Colin Firth as Prince Albert (the future King George VI, but then the Duke of York and known to his family as "Bertie") facing the ordeal of making his first radio broadcast. To add to the strain, the duke must deliver the address in a stadium before a large crowd. However, his words come only haltingly, causing embarrassment for all present. Not shown but later referenced in the film is the fact that in the crowd was Lionel Logue (Geoffrey Rush), a speech therapist recently transplanted from Australia.

All this took place in 1925, but Seidler brings the speech disaster forward 10 years to the eve of the abdication crisis, which resulted in the duke unexpectedly being transformed into a king when his brother Edward VIII stepped aside. The compression of events, although understandable, requires a slew of historical alterations to explain the back story.

The duke's stammer derived in part from the verbal abuse he received as a child from his father, King George V (Michael Gambon). To indicate this, Seidler concocts a scene showing the adult Bertie still being hectored by his father, and it is only after this that he agrees to see Logue.

Much of the early part of the film is taken up with Logue's struggle to win the duke's trust. The therapist succeeds partly by trickery and partly because of continued prompting by Bertie's wife, the Duchess of York (Helena Bonham Carter). After achieving a "breakthrough" with his patient and following Edward's abdication in 1936, Logue helps prepare the new king for the ordeal of the coronation ceremony. That hurdle cleared, the film culminates with the therapist coaching Bertie through another historic moment: his broadcast to the British Empire at the start of World War II with an approving Churchill (Timothy Spall) looking on.

In reality, the duke first sought treatment from Logue in 1926, and, contrary to the film, the two hit it off immediately. Logue wrote in a note later published in the king's official biography that Bertie left their first meeting brimming with confidence. After just two months of treatment, the duke's improvement was significant enough for him to begin making successful royal tours with all the public speaking that entailed. George V was so delighted that Bertie rapidly became his favored son and preferred heir.

In interviews, Seidler has been ambiguous about what sources he consulted in writing the script. The various biographies of George VI all tell of the king's relationship with Logue. This includes the official biography published in 1958. John Wheeler-Bennett, the royal biographer personally selected by the king's widow, was himself a former patient of Logue's and so wrote about the episode with great emotion.

It remains unclear, though, to what extent sources not available to scholars or the public played a role in the final shape of the film. Seidler has said that Logue's son offered 30 years ago to show him his father's notebooks, provided the king's widow agreed. But when Seidler wrote Queen Elizabeth, the Queen Mother, he was told that she found it too painful to remember the old anguish and begged that he wait until she had passed away.

Although the Queen Mother died in 2002, filmmakers said they were provided with Logue's diaries, notes and letters only shortly before filming began. Seidler has not specified how material from Logue's records was used, but he has said that research guided him to the conclusion that Logue utilized Freud's "talking cure" approach. Thus, by reading up on the king's life, Seidler used what he terms "informed imagination" to create the film's therapy scenes.

Seidler also drew on personal experience: He himself stammered as a child, and it was this that led him to an interest in George VI. From what he has said about his own successful treatment, Seidler indicates that he projected that experience into his fabrication about Logue having to work patiently to gain Bertie's trust. This liberty with the truth certainly gives the film more dramatic interest.

There are many other instances of artistic license in "The King's Speech." For example, Bertie chose his regal cognomen, George, out of respect for his father and not as the film has it because Churchill suggested that Albert sounded "too German." Another dramatic fantasy occurs when the Archbishop of Canterbury (Derek Jacobi) breathlessly revealed that Logue was not in fact a doctor. In reality, Logue's credentials were never misrepresented. Bertie always referred to him as "Mr. Logue" or simply "Logue." Logue's grandchildren recently came forward to say that their grandfather never used Christian names with the king at all – despite the movie making a strong point that the future king bristled at being called "Bertie" by Logue.

license AE
licence BE

As for Hitchens' allegations, they are much ado about nothing. Churchill's support of Edward VIII owed more to his near-medieval reverence for the monarchy than it did to the individual occupying the throne. In supporting the appeasement policies of Chamberlain, George VI acted in harmony with the overwhelming majority of the British population across the political spectrum. As a combat veteran of World War I, the king was as anxious as his subjects to avoid a second conflict by any promising means. George VI was also at one with most Britons in remaining skeptical about Churchill as prime minister until the great man had proved himself.

skeptical AE
sceptical BE

Hitchens will get a second chance to scrutinize moviedom's portrayal of Edward VIII and George VI this year, when Madonna's film "W.E." – about Wallis Simpson and Edward – hits theaters. He's probably already stocking up on pencils.

Where does Freeman identify artistic licence and what does he point out to be historically correct? How does he judge the changes Seidler made?

Component 6

Post-viewing activities

In diesem letzten Abschnitt wird ein besonderes Augenmerk auf die Rede von König George VI gelegt. Im Anschluss werden *post-viewing tasks* vorgestellt, die mit Rezensionen, den Schauspielern und dem Filmscript verschiedene inhaltliche Bereiche ansprechen und somit nicht chronologisch behandelt werden müssen. Abschließend wird der Fokus noch einmal geöffnet und auf die heutige Rolle der Monarchie in Großbritannien gelenkt.

6.1 The King speaks

Der Höhepunkt des Films ist die von King George VI ohne erkennbares Stottern vorgetragene Rede zum Kriegseintritt Großbritanniens. Seine Nervosität und Versagensängste in der vorangehenden Szene, die durch das Fluchen und Singen noch komische Elemente beinhaltet, betonen die Ernsthaftigkeit und Tragik der Radioansprache umso mehr. Es ist besonders aufschlussreich, eine Kopie des Redetextes mit den Anmerkungen von Lionel Logue zu Pausen und Änderungen zu betrachten, der erneut die Nähe des Films zu historischen Tatsachen verdeutlicht (***Copy 28***). Darüber hinaus kann auch die Rede unter den Textanalyseaspekten der *political speeches* untersucht werden, wobei hier als Vertonung nicht die Filmversion, sondern die Audiodatei der Originalrede von King George VI aus dem Jahr 1939 herangezogen werden sollte (http://www.bbc.co.uk/archive/ww2outbreak/7918.shtml). Der nicht ganz einfache Text der Rede, geschrieben unter dem Briefkopf des Buckingham Palace, verdeutlicht, dass George VI das Eingreifen Großbritanniens in den Konflikt als Maßnahme zur Friedenssicherung bzw. -wiederherstellung sieht.

> How does George VI address his nation "in this grave hour"? What does he say? Listen to the speech (http://www.bbc.co.uk/archive/ww2outbreak/7918.shtml) and analyse the tone. Compare the notes made by Logue with the recording. What do you notice?

Lösungsvorschlag/möglicher Tafelanschrieb:

Die Ergebnisse sind hier textchronologisch dargelegt. Innerhalb der Analyse wäre selbstverständlich auch eine Systematisierung nach *rhetoric devices* sinnvoll.

content	devices
opens by telling his peoples in the United Kingdom and overseas that he commiserates with them and feels close to them	• use of the first-person singular pronoun "I" and possessive pronoun "my": George VI as King is responsible for his people • direct address ("for each one of you", "speak to you myself" "every household"): each single person is affected by what he says as they will have to fight this war together
stresses the importance of this special moment in time	• choice of words: "grave"; "most fateful" (superlative)
points out that unfortunately all the attempts to keep the peace have failed	• use of the first-person plural pronoun, i.e. inclusive pronoun ("For the second time in the lives of most of us we are at war"): creates a feeling of community, stresses the common past and then reveals the terrible news • repetition/hyperbole ("over and over again") stresses the fruitless attempts • contrast between "ourselves" and "those who are now our enemies", nevertheless the use of "now" points out that the others are not generally evil, but that the notions of friends and enemies are only true in this new state of war • "a principle […] fatal to any civilized order in the world" has not yet been elaborated on; this follows in the next paragraph and thus, by repeating the word "principle", he links the different parts of his speech
war has become necessary because the set rules have been violated by a state (Germany) which presumes that "might is right"	• explanation why "the principle" is to be condemned with the help of words with a negative connotation ("selfish", "to disregard", "force against", "primitive") culminating in the rhyming slogan "might is right"
consequently, Britain cannot refuse her help and has to act to defend peace, justice and liberty	• if-clause to show the dangers • enumeration/gradation in three steps: freedom of the United Kingdom and the Commonwealth would be endangered, the peoples of the world would live in fear, and even the hopes of peace, justice and liberty would be in vain • image of "the bondage of fear" stresses worse restraints than those of having to fight in a war • absolute statements ("the ultimate issue", "all that we hold dear") show that he and his people ("we") have no choice but "to meet the challenge"; by phrasing it like this he states his call to participate in this war not only as the logical consequence but also as something ultimately positive (a "challenge" is something you take on to overcome and prevail)
aiming at the "high purpose" of "the world's order and peace" will demand a lot from his peoples, but he asks them to stand together in the "dark days ahead", not to lose their faith and to trust in God's help	• direct personal message in shorter sentences ("I now call my people", "I ask them"), this time evading a direct address (no second-person pronoun) when describing the future hardships • return to the first-person plural pronoun ("we", "us") when referring the people and the cause to God • alliteration "dark days" to stress how bad it will turn out • alliteration "service or sacrifice" • reference to God; "we shall prevail"

content	devices
stresses his statements	• parallelism "In this grave hour", "For the second time in the lives of most of us", "We have been forced", "We have tried to find" • anaphora "we have" • enumerations ("all hopes of settled peace and of security, of justice and liberty, among nations"; "we ourselves hold dear, and of the world order and peace") show what is at stake • tricolon "to stand calm and firm and unite"

tone: serious, grave, firm, sometimes hesitating (on the background of his speech, knowing about his defect it is not clear whether the sometimes long pauses are due to his pronunciation difficulties or whether they are caused by the emotional situation and difficult content of the message he has to deliver)
notes: Logue's notes show that they on the one hand facilitate the pronunciation and flow of the speech (the insertion of a comma after "over and over again we" indicating a pause, the change from "If it" into "If this principle" and from "summon" into "call") and on the other hand stress important words and parts. The slight pauses before meaningful last words in different sentences ("at war", "in vain", "that might is right", "in danger") add much to the grave effect.

In einem weiteren Schritt können die Schülerinnen und Schüler auch die vergleichsweise kurze Ansprache von Premierminister Chamberlain zum Kriegseintritt hören und hinsichtlich Inhalt, Form und Ton mit der von King George VI vergleichen. Die Ansprache kommt im Film selbst vor, kann aber auch als Audiodatei im Internet gehört werden. (http://www.bbc.co.uk/schoolradio/subjects/history/ww2clips/speeches/chamberlain_declares_war). Diese Aufgabe ist besonders interessant, da Chamberlain hier die sachliche Rolle des Premierministers zukommt, während George VI dem Volk in emotionaler und persönlicher Art und Weise begegnet, wie es seine Funktion als Monarch erfordert. Falls die Ansprache im Filmkontext untersucht wird, werden neben der eigentlichen Textaussage auch die Reaktionen der gezeigten Charaktere auf diese Nachricht analysiert.

German DVD
1:30:13–1:30:55

English DVD
1:29:44–1:30:32

Listen to Prime Minister Chamberlain's radio announcement (http://www.bbc.co.uk/schoolradio/subjects/history/ww2clips/speeches/chamberlain_declares_war). Compare it to the speech given by George VI the same day.

Lösungsvorschlag:

Chamberlain's announcement: Though speaking in a very grave tone as well, he explains the entry into the war more factually, first telling the people where he is (i.e. that he is still in London) and then explaining the British ultimatum and its consequence, namely the state of war with Germany. The Prime Minister fulfills his (unpleasant) duty of informing the British people, but without the explicit personal note that the King's message had as he is just the head of the government whereas King George VI is to be seen as the head of the nation and of the whole Commonwealth.

Reactions: The Logues: listening to the radio announcement; quiet and shocked faces; Logue's hand on his wife's shoulder when "the state of war" is mentioned should comfort her, but the tilt of his face shows that he is as worried as she is; calm, slow music underlines the sad atmosphere; final close-ups of the faces of Lionel and his son show their devastation and helplessness.

6.2 Reviews

Nach der eingehenden Behandlung des Films bieten sich nun neben der selbstständigen Bewertung des Gesehenen verschiedene Filmrezensionen an, die diverse Aspekte von *The King's Speech* betonen.
Um neben dem textanalytischen Herangehen auch die kommunikativen und sprachmittelnden Kompetenzen der Lerngruppe zu stärken, soll im Folgenden eine Rezension aus dem deutschen Sprachraum („Eure Majestät, Ihr stottert", ***Copy 29***) ins Englische übertragen werden. Hier können einerseits die wesentlichen inhaltlichen Aussagen, andererseits für leistungsstärkere Schülerinnen und Schüler auch die sprachlich-stilistischen Besonderheiten in die englische Sprache übersetzt werden, um anschließend zu den bewerteten Aspekten persönlich Stellung zu nehmen. Dieses Vorgehen hat den Vorteil, in der folgenden Phase eine realistische Gesprächssituation zu schaffen, in der sich jeder einzelne individuell einbringen und äußern kann.

1. Read the text in your own language.
2. Sum up Pilarczyk's opinion on the film in English. (Try to stick to her way of writing).
3. Comment on her opinion.

Die Erarbeitungsphase der Sprachmittlung kann um eine binnendifferenzierende Aufgabenstellung erweitert werden, indem eine zweite Rezension in englischer Sprache („The critics are wrong: The King's Speech s-s-sucks", ***Copy 30***) hinzugenommen wird, sodass für einige Schülerinnen und Schüler die Sprachmittlungsphase entfällt. Je nach Leistungsniveau des Kurses und Arbeitsphase können optional die Annotationen den Schülerinnen und Schülern zur Verfügung gestellt werden.

1. Read the text and sum up Marx's opinion on the film.
2. Comment on his opinion.

Inhaltlich werden hier im Gegensatz zur ersten *review* ausschließlich negative Aspekte angemerkt, sodass die Schülerinnen und Schüler ihre eigene Argumentation in einem sich anschließenden Dialog mit einem Partner aus der Sprachmittlungsgruppe erweitern bzw. abgrenzen können.

Compare the opinion given in your text with a partner who has read the other text. Note down the new aspects/arguments.

Aufgrund der individuellen Rezeption können die Dialogpartner mehrfach wechseln (*double circle*/Kugellagermethode).

Form a double circle. The mediation group sits in the outer circle, the other group in the inner circle. Inform you partner about the opinion stated in your text.
To change partners the outer circle moves three places clockwise.

Denkbar ist auch, die erste Phase in arbeitsgleichen Gruppen zu belassen, sodass die Partner ihre Zusammenfassungen erst abgleichen können, bevor sie die Ergebnisse einem anderen Partner vorstellen.

Find a partner who worked on the same text and compare your results.

Die in den Rezensionen erwähnten wertenden Aspekte werden im Folgenden zusammenfassend aufgeführt.

Eure Majestät, Ihr stottert	**The King's Speech s-s-sucks**
⊕ mitreißendes Drama	⊙ Historical inaccuracies
⊕ gekonntes Crescendo; fängt als leichte Kömodie an und steigert sich fast unmerklich zu einem mitreißenden Drama	⊕ Firth's performance
⊕ skurrile Einschläge	⊖ bland, predictable and ordinary film
⊕ Rush's närrisches Treiben; Firth's Sprödheit	⊖ childishly unbelievable
⊕ Danny Cohen fängt Spiel und Streit zwischen den Männern gekonnt ein	⊕ great acting
⊕ opulente Ausstattung	⊖ characters are thinly and clumsily drawn to the point of caricature and contradiction, e. g. Logue and Bertie
⊖ Streben nach Versöhnlichkeit: Chamberlains Appeasement-Politik wirkt so, als hätte er sie allein vertreten und König Edwards VIII faschistische Tendenzen werden heruntergespielt	⊖ odd zany montage of therapist and patient ... as if behaving like an idiot will somehow cure him of sounding like one
⊕ intimer Film	⊖ no single moment of dialogue that might tell us what this movie is about, or would even score a place on a cheap inspirational desk calendar
	⊖ that it won the Oscar for Best Original Screenplay is perplexing, being that the most moving lines by far come from King George's actual speech from 1939

Legende: ⊕ positiv; ⊖ negativ, ⊙ neutral

Im Anschluss an den Austausch mit (verschiedenen) Partnern sollen die Schülerinnen und Schüler selbst eine Rezension verfassen, in der sie ihre positiven und negativen Kritikpunkte schriftlich darlegen. Falls das Schreiben von Rezensionen in der Lerngruppe bisher noch nicht thematisiert worden ist, können die Schülerinnen und Schüler die Aufgabe mit der folgenden Anleitung auch selbstständig (in einer Hausaufgabe) bearbeiten.

How to write a film review

Title: The easiest solution is to take the title of the film, but you can think of something different (funny, critical, ...), too.

Introduction: You can begin with information about the film (e.g. awards, Oscars) and/or the director (e.g. awards, former movies). Also quotes and/or anecdotes may catch the readers' attention. You can also describe what you expected from the film.

Main part: Provide a **brief summary** of the plot. Make sure that your summary makes sense to a reader who does *not* know the movie. Do *not* refer to specific scenes. Is the plot interesting, believable or rather predictable?

Present the **main actors and their characters** and say something about their performance. If you like you may give reasons why you identify with a certain character. Are the actors believable and sympathetic?

State your **opinion** of the movie and give reasons for it. What are its strengths and weaknesses? Support your opinion with references to specific scenes. Is the **soundtrack** appropriate?
What is special about the film? Does it have a specific message?

Conclusion: Either recommend the film or advise against watching it. Is this only a film for a certain target group (teenagers, women, young men, ...)?

adapted from: http://www.jochenenglish.de/?p=7161 [13 02 2013]

6.3 The actors and their roles

Besonders aufgrund von Colin Firths überragender schauspielerischer Leistung in seiner Rolle als King George VI, für die er verdient mit dem *Academy Award* ausgezeichnet wurde, stellt seine persönliche Sichtweise seiner Rolle eine Bereicherung für den Unterricht dar. Das vorliegende Interview (***Copy 31***) wurde insofern gekürzt, als dass die Problematik der Altersbeschränkung des Films in den USA aufgrund der vulgären Sprache ausgelassen wurde. Falls diese Thematik im Unterricht besprochen werden soll, findet man das vollständige Interview unter http://screencrave.com/2010-11-24/interview-colin-firth-talks-the-kings-speech/. Der Einsatz des Textes bietet sich wegen seines Umfangs als Hausaufgabe an.

1. What does Firth say about Bertie's isolation due to his role as a prince/king?
2. Sum up what Firth says about speech impediments.
3. What does Firth think about winning the Oscar?

Lösungsvorschläge zu *Copy 31*:

1. Firth believes it is difficult to know as he is neither a member of the Royal Family nor a person who has lived at the same time. To him isolation is everywhere and lots of people hide behind walls. Bertie's barriers (the protocol, his titles etc.) can be seen as metaphors for other walls.
2. In Firth's opinion Bertie has not overcome his stammer in the film. He has just come to terms with it and does not let himself be restricted unduly by it. He himself realized that after training to stammer for the film, he sometimes fell back into this pattern. In general he has great esteem for actors and other people who have managed to overcome their stammer.

3. Firth likes getting attention for his performance as King George VI and would welcome whatever he gets but he wants to wait for the film to come out.

In der folgenden ***Copy 32*** kommen neben Firth weitere Schaupieler zu Wort. Diese kürzeren Texte können ergänzend oder alternativ zu ***Copy 31*** behandelt werden.

Summarize why the actors were fascinated by the film, their roles or by the persons they represent in the film.

Lösungsvorschlag zu *Copy 32*:

- As Firth, of course, could not spend some time with a real king as actors usually spend some time in the job they have to portray, he prepared himself by reading letters and biographies and then he tried to embody Bertie's characteristic wryness.
- Bonham Carter liked the two different sides of Queen Elizabeth as she represented the charming, typical Edwardian woman on the outside and, behind it, her strong character.
- Rush especially likes the fascinating story of two very unlike men, being of different status, from different countries and different backgrounds, and their relationship.
- Pearce had always known what a fascinating character he would play, but just tried to be as good as possible as he didn't have much camera time.
- Spall states that the film was written the way people talked at that time.

Der Einsatz von Bildern im Englischunterricht eignet sich in Zeiten der Bilderfluten besonders, da der Blick der Schüler geschärft und ihre Kritikfähigkeit erhöht wird. Werden Bilder häufig als Sprechanlässe im Rahmen von Unterrichtseinstiegen eingesetzt, bietet es sich – vor allem in Grundkursen – an dieser Stelle jedoch an, einen Cartoon über Colin Firths Haltung seiner Rolle gegenüber (***Copy 33***) in einem ausführlicheren Schritt zu analysieren. Cartoons allgemein eignen sich hier hervorragend, da Cartoonisten häufig einfache Objekte oder Symbole zur Darstellung genereller Konzepte verwenden. Auch sind die Illustrationen häufig karikiert und daher übertrieben, sodass es den Schülerinnen und Schülern leichter fällt, den jeweiligen Sachverhalt zu analysieren als bei der Arbeit mit Texten.
Der vorliegende Cartoon ermöglicht eine kritische Auseinandersetzung mit Firths Selbstverständnis und der Einschätzung seiner Rolle, für die er einen *Academy Award* erhalten hat.

Lösungsvorschlag zu *Copy 33*:

1. The release of the film "The King's Speech" inspired the cartoonist.
2. Colin Firth is portrayed in the cartoon. His head and half his torso are shown. Firth's face is friendly, smiling; he is holding his shirt open so that the viewer can see his bare breast showing the Union Jack.
3. Apart from Firth there's a To-Do List presented in the cartoon, which is supposed to be Firth's list. The list shows that Firth acted his role so well that he must change the billing now and must inform his fellow actress Bonham Carter that she is not the real queen.
   The symbol of the Union Jack stands for patriotism.
4. The cartoon makes fun of the hype around Colin Firth and his role as King George VI.
5. individual answers

How to interpret a cartoon

Step 1: Introduce the analysis by stating the title or caption of the cartoon, the name of the artist and of the magazine or newspaper where it was published and the date of publication.
Step 2: Describe what you see in the picture (people, setting, objects, colours,...). State what the main topic is and then explain what you can see in the centre and in the background.
Step 3: Analyse the artist's intention. What message is conveyed? What is criticized and how successfully is this done?
Step 4: State your personal opinion.

useful expressions:
The cartoon depicts ...; In the foreground/ In the background, one can see ...; The atmosphere is rather ...; The ... symbolizes ...; The artist wants to point out ...; In my opinion ...

6.4 The screenplay

Als Abschluss der Beschäftigung mit dem Film kann eine Stellungnahme von David Seidler (***Copy 34***) dienen, die seine Motivation für die Entstehung des Filmscripts beleuchtet. Dieser Text ist als Hintergrundinformation für die Schülerinnen und Schüler sehr interessant, da Seidler selbst in seiner Kindheit stotterte und durch die Reden King Georges VI motiviert wurde, seine Sprachstörung zu überwinden. Auch die Tatsache, dass Seidler schon lange plante, Berties Leben zu verfilmen und dies für *Queen Elizabeth, the Queen Mother* zu schmerzhaft war, stellen eine wertvolle Ergänzung für den Unterricht dar.

1. What was the motivation for Seidler to write about King George VI?
2. Why did Seidler wait so long to make the film?

Lösungsvorschlag zu *Copy 34*:

1. Being of Jewish origin David Seidler was evacuated from London to America at the beginning of World War II. The journey on the ship was such a traumatic experience that Seidler started to stutter at the age of three. As a child he listened to King George VI's addresses to his people and became motivated to overcome his stammer like the king had managed to do.
2. Seidler wrote a letter to *Queen Elizabeth, the Queen Mother,* who asked him not to write the screenplay during her lifetime as those memories were painful to her.

6.5 Is the monarchy still relevant?

Nach einem ausführlichen Einblick in das Leben, die Aufgaben sowie die Probleme der royalen Familie kurz vor dem Zweiten Weltkrieg bietet sich nun eine abschließende Betrachtung der heutigen Situation der Monarchie in Großbritannien an. Je nachdem, wie ausführlich ***Component 2*** behandelt wurde, sind die heutigen Mitglieder der britschen Königsfamilie der Lerngruppe bereits bekannt (s. 2.3). Als Überleitung auf die heutige Situation könnten als Sprechanlass die beiden cartoons (***Copy 36***) oder das offizielle Hochzeitsfoto vom Duke und der Duchess of Cambridge (http://www.princeofwales.gov.uk/newsandgallery/gallery/the_wedding_of_prince_william_and_catherine_middleton_1988728899_1085621233.html) oder ***Copy 35*** dienen. Die Schüler können, angeregt durch den Bildimpuls, ihr Wissen über die Mitglieder der Königsfamilie rekapitulieren und anschließend die Frage aufwerfen, ob die Monarchie in der heutigen Zeit in Großbritannien noch von Bedeutung ist.

Lösungsvorschlag zu *Copy 36:*

In the first cartoon a patriotic couple is watching the Royal Wedding and is wondering why they are not invited as they are paying for the celebrations. The cartoonist wants to criticise the fact that the tax payers must support the Royal Family and their fancy lifestyle.
In the second cartoon you can see extinct animals in a museum who are watching William and Kate driving by in a carriage on their wedding day. The cartoonist wants to stress that there is no reason why the UK still sticks to this old-fashioned, outdated institution.

In diskussionsfreudigen Kursen liegt zur Beantwortung der Frage *Is the monarchy still relevant?* die Methode *Think Pair Share* nahe, mit der die Schüler gemäß ihres eigenen Standpunkts in drei Schritten Argumente sammeln und einander vorstellen können (siehe ***Copy 35***).
Zunächst kann an dieser Stelle ein Meinungsbild abgefragt werden (z. B. mithilfe von gelben, grünen und roten Karten oder Schildern mit *Yes, No, undecided*). Es ist wichtig, dass alle Schülerinnen und Schüler gleichzeitig bzw. unabhängig voneinander ihren Standpunkt vertreten, sodass sie nicht durch die Ansicht einzelner Meinungsführer beeinflusst werden.
Anschließend sammeln die Schülerinnen und Schüler im ersten Schritt in Einzelarbeit Argumente, die ihre Position unterstützen. Im nächsten Schritt vergleichen sie ihre Ergebnisse mit einem Partner, der der gleichen Auffassung war (noch unentschlossene Schüler könnten für beide Seiten Argumente sammeln). Im letzten Schritt kommen jeweils zwei Paare mit unterschiedlichen Auffassungen zusammen und diskutieren in ihrer Vierergruppe die Frage, ob die Monarchie noch relevant ist. Zum Abschluss wird erneut ein Meinungsbild abgefragt und das neue Ergebnis mit dem ersten Ergebnis verglichen.
Als Zusatzaufgabe bietet sich die Möglichkeit an, einen zusätzlichen Text zu lesen und ergänzende Argumente herauszuschreiben (je nach Position des Schülers ***Copy 37*** [Yes] und ***Copy 38*** [No].)

Lösungsvorschlag:

Shields	Blackburn
has changed (l. 3)	took more than 200 years to change sexism (ll. 2 ff.)
modernising (l. 4)	House of Lords was modernised, monarchy wasn't (ll. 7 f.)
gender equality (ll. 11 ff.)	modern multi-cultural Britain isn't represented by a religiously discriminatory monarchy system (ll. 12 ff.)
combine tradition with new generation (ll. 14 f.)	undemocratic (l. 15)
more accessible (ll. 18 f.)	costs too much tax money (ll. 29 ff.)
we can relate to them (ll. 20 ff.)	rich, but not self-sufficient (ll. 28 f.)
face of Britain (l. 28)	embarrassing (ll. 31 f.)
history and tradition (ll. 33 ff.)	less public duties, but costs more (ll. 35 ff.)

In Kursen, die evtl. weniger Vorwissen über das politsche System und die Vor- und Nachteile der Monarchie mitbringen, kann die Methode *Think Pair Share* insofern abgewandelt werden, als dass die Schüler im ersten Schritt arbeitsteilig die Texte auf ***Copy 37*** und ***Copy 38*** lesen, sich im zweiten Schritt mit einem Partner, der den gleichen Text gelesen hat, zusammensetzen, um die Argumente zu vergleichen, und im letzten Schritt – wie oben in einer Vierergruppe – aus den unterschiedlichen Positionen heraus diskutieren.
Eine mögliche differenzierende Aufgabe wäre hier, die gegebenen Aspekte um eigene Argumente zu ergänzen. Des Weiteren kann – ggf. in einer zusammenfassenden Hausaufgabe – abschließend die Positionen des deutschen und des britischen Staatsoberhaupts verglichen und eine begründete Stellungnahme verfasst werden, die die Vor- und Nachteile bzw. die persönlich bevorzugte Form darlegt.

1. Add your own arguments to the list.
2. Comment on whether you would rather have a King or Queen or a President in Germany.

Lösungsvorschlag zu *Copy 37* und *38*:

YES	NO
a political head of state who is above parties	hereditary head of state does not necessarily denote intelligence (as likely to produce a complete idiot as it is a well-read, intelligent monarch)
has the best interests of the nation at heart rather than other considerations, e.g. party interests	monarch represents class system and not equality
regarded as archaic but brings a lot of money as tourists are interested in palaces and souvenirs	a monarch does not have any political influence anymore
monarchy can lead public opinion; although above party politics, modern members of the British Royal Family have proved able to raise important, sometimes unpopular issues that would have otherwise been ignored, such as Prince Charles's work for the environment and Diana's work with AIDS and landmines	
links with other states	
creates a feeling of nationhood	
members of the British Royal Family, e.g. Queen Mum, Prince William, are popular	
everybody knows the respective royal families, an elected president is often not well-known	

2. individuelle Schülerantworten

Original copy of King George VI's speech

BUCKINGHAM PALACE

In this grave hour, perhaps the most fateful in our history, I send to every household of my peoples, both at home and overseas, this message, spoken with the same depth of feeling for each one of you as if I were able to cross your threshold and speak to you myself.

For the second time in the lives of most of us we are at war. Over and over again, we have tried to find a peaceful way out of the differences between my ~~Government~~ ourselves and those who are now our enemies. But it has been in vain. We have been forced into a conflict. For we are called, with our allies, to meet the challenge of a principle which, if it were to prevail, would be fatal to any civilized order in the world.

It is the principle which permits a State, in the

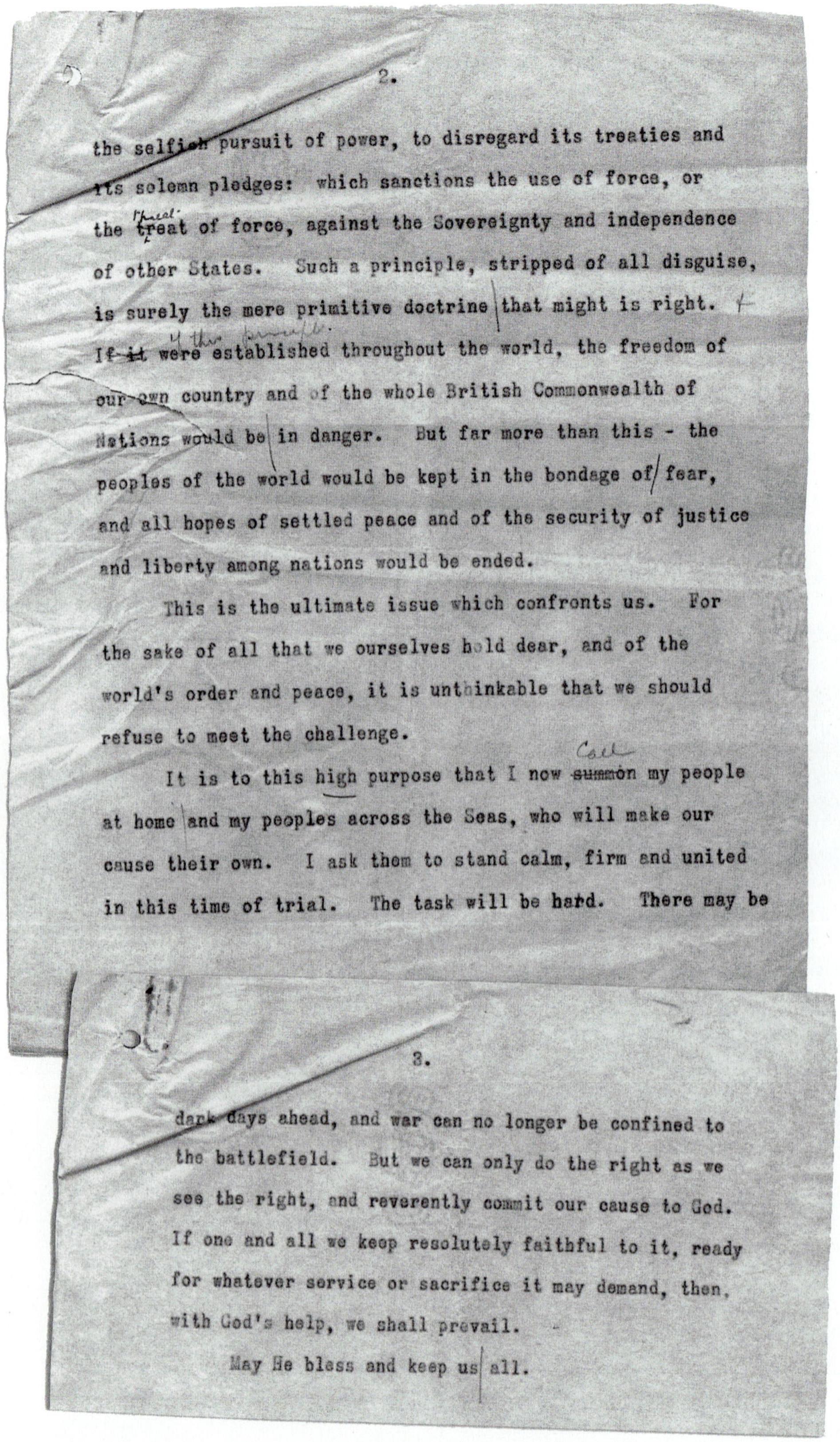

2.

the selfish pursuit of power, to disregard its treaties and its solemn pledges: which sanctions the use of force, or the threat of force, against the Sovereignty and independence of other States. Such a principle, stripped of all disguise, is surely the mere primitive doctrine that might is right. If this principle were established throughout the world, the freedom of our own country and of the whole British Commonwealth of Nations would be in danger. But far more than this - the peoples of the world would be kept in the bondage of fear, and all hopes of settled peace and of the security of justice and liberty among nations would be ended.

This is the ultimate issue which confronts us. For the sake of all that we ourselves hold dear, and of the world's order and peace, it is unthinkable that we should refuse to meet the challenge.

It is to this high purpose that I now call my people at home and my peoples across the Seas, who will make our cause their own. I ask them to stand calm, firm and united in this time of trial. The task will be hard. There may be

3.

dark days ahead, and war can no longer be confined to the battlefield. But we can only do the right as we see the right, and reverently commit our cause to God. If one and all we keep resolutely faithful to it, ready for whatever service or sacrifice it may demand, then, with God's help, we shall prevail.

May He bless and keep us all.

Neville Chamberlain (Prime Minister 1937–1940):

"I am speaking to you from the Cabinet Room of 10 Downing Street. This morning the British Ambassador in Berlin handed the German government a final note, stating that unless we heard from them – by 11 o'clock – that they were prepared at once to withdraw their troops from Poland, a state of war would exist between us […]; I have to tell you now that no such undertaking has been received and that, consequently, this country is at war with Germany."

Source: http://www.bbc.co.uk/schoolradio/subjects/history/ww2clips/speeches/chamberlain_declares_war [13 02 2013]

Hannah Pilarczyk: „Eure Majestät, Ihr stottert"

Mit zwölf Nominierungen ist „The King's Speech" der große Favorit bei den diesjährigen Oscars – zu Recht: Der Film ist ein mitreißendes Drama über den stotternden britischen Thronfolger Albert. Der muss erst seine Stimme finden, bevor er regieren kann.

[...] In „The King's Speech" spielt Firth den stotternden Prinzen Albert, den unfreiwillige Pausen beim Sprechen und bewusste Zurückhaltung beim Entscheiden zum unwahrscheinlichen Helden machen. Auch er selbst sieht sich nicht als König eines Landes, das bald in den Krieg ziehen wird – und schon gar nicht als begnadeter Rhetoriker, der mit Worten regiert. [...] Am Ende des Films wird er als König George VI. Großbritannien in den Zweiten Weltkrieg führen.

Wie es dazu kam, erzählen Regisseur Tom Hooper und Drehbuchautor David Seidler (beide ebenfalls Oscar-nominiert) in gekonntem Crescendo: „The King's Speech" fängt als leichte Komödie an und steigert sich fast unmerklich zu einem mitreißenden Drama.

Mit Tricks in die Praxis gelockt

Um ihrem Ehemann die Angst vor öffentlichen Reden zu nehmen, entschließt sich Elizabeth (Oscar-nominiert: Helena Bonham Carter), ihn zum Sprachtherapeuten zu schicken. Nur mit Tricks kann sie ihn in die schäbige Praxis von Lionel Logue (Geoffrey Rush – ja, auch nominiert) locken, nur mit Tricks kann der den widerspenstigen Patienten halten. Er setzt ihm Kopfhörer mit dröhnender Musik auf, dazu soll er aus „Hamlet" rezitieren, während Logue seine Worte mit dem Grammophon aufnimmt. Nach wenigen Versen gibt Albert entnervt auf und bricht die Therapie schon in der ersten Sitzung ab. Erst später, daheim auf dem Sofa, hört er sich die Aufnahme an. Auf der Schallplatte ist ein souveräner Redner zu hören, den die Musik wirkungsvoll von dem abgelenkt hat, was ihn am meisten stört – seine eigene Stimme. Am nächsten Tag ist er zurück in Logues Praxis.

Nur langsam entwickelt sich echtes Vertrauen zwischen Logue und Albert, viel später wird daraus auch Freundschaft. Zwischen den beiden Männern herrschen große Temperamentsunterschiede, die Rush und Firth mit sichtlichem Vergnügen spielen. Rushs Logue verführt mehr, als dass er heilt. Sich auf seinen Therapieansatz einzulassen, heißt, sich auch auf ihn als Menschen einzulassen. Was bei manchen skurrilen Einschlägen – wie etwa dem völlig unbegründeten Glauben, ein großer Schauspieler zu sein – nicht ganz leicht fällt.

Streben nach allumfassender Versöhnlichkeit

In Kontrast zu Rushs närrischem Treiben kann Firth ganz auf Sprödheit setzen. Sein Albert sitzt steif auf jedem Sofa und in jedem Sessel, sein Körper neigt sich gegen alle Achsen im Raum. Bis er innere und äußere Harmonie findet, muss noch einiges passieren – sowohl an sprachtherapeutischen Übungen als auch weltpolitischen Großlagen.

Danny Cohens Cinematografie fängt Spiel und Streit zwischen den Männern gekonnt ein, unterstützt von einer erwartbar opulenten Ausstattung. Mit dem wiederholten Wechsel der Perspektiven von unten und oben thematisiert Cohens außerdem die Schichtunterschiede zwischen ihnen. Damit überdeckt er leidlich die große Schwachstelle des Films – nämlich sein Streben nach allumfassender Versöhnlichkeit.

Chamberlains Appeasement-Politik gegenüber Hitler wird in „The King's Speech" zum Irrglauben eines einzelnen, schwachen Politikers. Die Nazi-Sympathien von Alberts Bruder und Vorgänger auf dem Thron, König Edward VIII., nehmen sich eher wie schlechte Manieren denn faschistische Tendenzen aus. [...]

Trotz der großen Themen ist „The King's Speech" aber zu allererst ein intimer Film. Er führt die Zuschauer in der ersten Hälfte so nahe an seine Hauptfiguren heran, dass ihre Erweiterung zu Personen der Zeitgeschichte in der zweiten Hälfte keinen Bruch bedeutet – im Gegenteil. Am Ende sieht man einem Sprachtherapie-Patienten über die Schulter, der soeben seinem Volk verkündet hat, dass man sich im Krieg mit Deutschland befindet. Vor ihm breitet sich eine Menschenmasse aus, die ihn für seine Worte feiert.

SPIEGEL ONLINE, Hannah Pilarczyk, 16.02.2011 10:24

http://www.spiegel.de/kultur/kino/oscar-favorit-the-king-s-speech-eure-majestaet-ihr-stottert-a-743386.html [07 12 2012]

1. Read the text in your own language.
2. Sum up Pilarczyk's opinion on the film in English.
3. Comment on her opinion.

Jack Marx Live Blog: "The critics are wrong: The King's Speech s-s-sucks", 3 March 2011

Last night, I relented to the implorations of the *Academy of Motion Picture Arts and Sciences* and almost the entire fraternity of movie critics by going to see *The King's Speech*. I am writing this today as both a message in a bottle and a warning, for while I do feel awfully lonely at present, I wouldn't wish for anyone else to join me in making such a lamentable mistake. *The King's Speech* is based on a true event, the moment when Australian speech therapist, Lionel Logue, was employed by King George VI (affectionately known as "Bertie") to help eradicate a debilitating stutter from which he had suffered all his life. Its historical inaccuracies, of which there are many, don't concern me – the world of motion pictures has long declared itself an opponent of exactitude, and there's no point in arguing with a determined liar. What confounds me about *The Kings Speech* is that, with the exception of Colin Firth's performance, it is a thoroughly bland, predictable and ordinary film that has somehow managed to convince everyone it is none of those things. [...]
But what makes *The King's Speech* so irritating is that it is so childishly unbelievable. It begins with the characters themselves which, behind the great acting that presents them, are thinly and clumsily drawn to the point of caricature and contradiction. Bertie rages furiously at Logue one moment and, the very next, meekly inquires as to what foolish thing the therapist might be up to next – behaviour that services dramatic expediency, but which would seem to suggest the King not only stammers, but is borderline schizophrenic. Logue is no better – at one point, having spent the entire film expressing his complete disregard for royal protocol, Logue is seen to be literally chasing Bertie through a park, crabbing up beside him and declaring, "You could be king!", with all the wide-eyed excitement of some hopeful boob from a Lotto commercial, a ludicrous reaction from a man who not only cares little for the trappings of royalty, but who knows full well of his patient's complete ambivalence toward the throne. [...]
[W]e are treated to the odd zany montage of therapist and patient getting down to business; Bertie dancing like a twit around the room, shouting "bugger, buggerty, buggerty, f**k, f**k, arse", or lying on the floor reading aloud while Elizabeth sits on his tummy and bounces up and down – as if merely behaving like an idiot will somehow cure him of sounding like one. One might have thought that a movie whose very premise lay in the art of speech would have been ripe for the sort of monologue that's worth remembering, something as elevating as Al Pacino's soliloquy to near-beaten footballers in *Any Given Sunday*, or Danny DeVito's deeply introspective rumination upon the nature of "character" in *The Big Kahuna* (films that didn't get within coo-ee of an Oscar nomination). But there is nothing like that in *The King's Speech*, no single moment of dialogue that might tell us what this movie has been about, or would even score a place on a cheap inspirational desk calendar. That it won the Oscar for Best Original Screenplay is perplexing, being that the most moving lines by far come from King George's actual speech from 1939, which, when it finally arrives at the end of *The King's Speech*, is a breath of fresh air after so much pointless bickering and cracking wise.
[I]f you laugh at the humour in McDonalds commercials, or at the idea of the Queen doing something as commonplace as a poo; [...] if the person you'd most like to sit next to on a plane is either the Dalai Lama or Nelson Mandela; if you're into *X Factor, Packed To The Rafters*, the Sunday papers and Will and Kate's wedding; if you're a critic in search of fans, or indeed if you're eight or eighty years old, then you might get a kick out of *The King's Speech*.

to relent *nachgeben*
debilitating inhibiting
to confound to irritate
boob *Dussel*
zany crazy, stupid
cooee *Rufweite*

Jack Marx Live Blog: "The critics are wrong: The King's Speech s-s-sucks, News Ltd – News.com.au 03/03/2011

1. Read the text and sum up Marx's opinion on the film.
2. Comment on his opinion.

Interview: Colin Firth Talks The King's Speech

[…] The film won the top prize at the 2010 Toronto International Film Festival and has many more awards on its way. We were lucky enough to have a chance to speak with Firth about his performance in the film, taking on such a challenging role, the obstacles the film is facing with the important albeit foul language in the film and much more …

albeit despite

Taking on a Speech Impediment:

Have you ever known anyone [who] stuttered and did you relate any of your performance to any real life experiences?

Colin Firth: I grew up with people who stammered. There seemed to be more […] than there are now, I wonder if there [are any figures] on that. I certainly knew people who did, yeah.

Did you know about the King's stammer prior to this film or any of the events surrounding it?

Firth: I knew about it, and that's it. All I knew was that he had a stammer.

Beyond the stammer is the issue about friendship and isolation, how could you relate to that as a person who is famous.

Firth: It's funny to say about a story about a member of the Royal Family when none of us [are] members of the Royal Family or could possibly know what that's like. Most of us were not around in 1937. There are all these things you could say – how could it possibly be universal? But I think, what [the film has] done, is taken an issue that applies to absolutely everybody and used this convention to heighten those things. Isolation is universal. It doesn't matter how close you are to your family, how many good friends you have, how perfect your marriage is – and most people are not ticking all those boxes. There's some level on which […] you can't be reached – we can't get inside each other's minds, hearts and souls. This is taking that reality, that truth and making a very extreme case out of it. If men protect themselves behind certain reserves against intimacy, let's take a man who not only does that – he's protected by high walls, titles, protocols, and make a therapist work through all those things, you could almost look at them as metaphors for barriers we all put up.

In the film it shows how he overcome his stutter…

Firth: He didn't overcome it. And I don't think the film shows him overcoming it. I think it shows him having an arrangement with it. Where he's not going to let it stop him from doing his job. You know, that last speech you still see him fighting, he has to have his therapist right there. He fights for every word. If you listen to the cadence (in his speech) it's a struggle, he has to break it up. That's the point! He was never cured – I tried to follow the cadences to some extent of the real speech. Some were more fluent than others, but you hear them very measured and broken up. You hear him going through three syllables ending on up phrases and then finding a down phrase and getting blocked again – that's a fight. Everyone who's sitting listening to it, The Queen, Churchill and the rest are on the edge of their seat til the end. So, he overcomes the debilitating fear of it – but he doesn't overcome the fact that he'll always have the obstacle.[…]

cadence tone

Tricks Behind the Performance:

What tricks did you use to get into that speech pattern and were you able to drop it at the end of the day?

Firth: I got a bit confused in my own speech patterns. There's very much a cult of actors telling you how deeply immersed they were and what it cost them – But, it's muscle memory. If you do an exercise often enough, your body will train yourself to do that exercise. If you train yourself to interfere with your rhythm of speech, something in your brain remembers that and follows it – If you're going around trying to promote "A Single Man" it sometimes come[s] to haunt you. And it did, that's not a stammer – that's my mind playing tricks on me. That's not a real stammer, I spoke to the head of the British Stammering Association a couple weeks ago, and he told me that the research shows now that there's a strong neurological component. It's not a psychological problem, there's something happening in the brain. It's physical. I asked if that meant that [the therapist in the film] is on the wrong track? He said "well no, because the therapy helps you come to an accommodation with the problem" – you learn not to be crushed by it, not to be disabled by it. You can find a way forward. There are wonderful, great actors who fought stammering …

pattern the way he speaks

James Earl Jones.

Firth: Yes! And there are a lot of others we could name. Politicians – Churchill has speech problems, really severe ones, which he says in the film. Not to mention writers,

Lewis Carroll, Somerset Moore. If you've lost the use of your legs, or you've lost your legs, the people who give us the inspiring and heroic stories are the people who triumph over it – not by getting their legs back but by living their [lives] that makes a virtue of what they've got and that's why we're so moved by it.

[...] *It was nice that certain scenes were left to just play and allow the stutter to take its time. How were those scenes for you?*

Firth: My first scene was the first scene with Logue [Rush's character] and it was an amazing baptism of fire, really. I hadn't really tried it out, we'd had three intense weeks of rehearsal where we were sitting there, Geoffrey, Tom Hooper, David Seidler, and myself honing that script. Really, really, really challenging every beat, finding what could be got out of it at its maximum, where the humor was to be highlighted ... but I couldn't sit in my own clothes in a hotel room with a script in my hand, really trying to go there. Film doesn't really allow for that kind of rehearsal in my experience. It wasn't until Tom put a camera on me, in that room that I thought, "I'm on, this is it now."

baptism of fire *Feuertaufe*

honing improving

And it's a very interesting thing how he shot it. He just decided he was going to make a huge commitment. You'd normally, I would think, start with a master shot. You've established everything, then refine things – he started with a mid-shot, just a single of me. And played an entire 10 minute scene. It's interesting, Tom will tell you, he committed to his cinematic style then and there. He had kept his options open up until that point. At the end of that day we thought, that's 10 percent of the movie we just did. He said that at the end of that day. It's rare that you have a scene long enough to say, we've got 10 weeks to go and we just shot 10 percent of this movie.
You can't break the convention – you can't suddenly say, "I'll do soft focus and dark lighting". In a way it was the same with me – I laid a character down, and it was wonderful to have that much of a run at it. It was like doing live theatre. And to have Geoffrey Rush and have his energy and his humor to bounce off gave me so much for nothing. What seemed to be an immense mountain to climb felt incredibly easy because I was in the hands not only of a director like that but an actor who energized me in every way I needed.

What's next for you?

Firth: I'm doing a movie called Tinker, Tailor, Soldier, Spy – it's a wonderful, wonderful novel which was a legendary, brilliant television series in the 1970's. I am playing a spy.

And the big "O" Question:

You should have won an Oscar last year and this year everyone is saying that you'll be winning an Oscar come next year? Would it be gratifying to get that kind of attention for this performance?

gratifying pleasant

Firth: It's gratifying to get attention for a performance. I'm not going to wish any of it away, talk as big as you like. I welcome all of it. But, the film has to come out. And all I can say about it right now is that if people are talking like that from the festivals and the few people who've seen it already, it's a wonderful start. It's code for it's a really good movie, at the moment, I completely welcome it.

Make sure to check out Colin Firth in The King's Speech starting this Friday, November 26th before he wins all the awards he has coming his way!

1. What does Firth say about Bertie's isolation due to his role as a prince/king?
2. Sum up what Firth says about speech impediments.
3. What does Firth think about winning the Oscar?

Actors about their roles in the film or the film

Colin Firth: "If I'm playing a doctor I might spend some time with a doctor going round the wards. But you can't hang around with the King, and the Queen is not going to give you a few days of her time. So you have to use secondary sources. And a lot of the biographers are rather enamoured of David (Edward VIII) as a character – it's easy to be enamoured with the charms, the romantic story there. And Bertie is often characterised as the shy, retiring, dull-witted brother. If you read anything he's written – a lot of what you saw in the film comes from his letters, the self-mockery, the wryness, the line where Logue says „You still stammered on the ‚w'" and Bertie says „I had to throw in a few extra ones so they knew it was me", that came from the diary, that was a quote from those two men. I found that in Logue's diary. I was looking through it and I thought we've got to have that in the film."

enamoured fascinated
dull-witted stupid

http://www.stammering.org/colinfirth.html [07 12 2012]

Helena Bonham Carter: "She was an expert public figure. She was born to be in that role, but she also knew that Albert wasn't. She was also great at creating her own brand, the image she projected – the soft, charming cloud of vagueness, very much of that time, an Edwardian woman. She played a sort of quite low status, almost geisha-like, with her head cocked to the side. But that was a pure veneer and underneath she was totally at odds, belied by her force of character. She wore the pants in the relationship."

cocked tilted
veneer *Fassade*

Vulture.com/Lorraine Cwelich

Geoffrey Rush: "Actually my primal response was that this would be tricky to film and would probably have no viable commercial life but that it was a fantastic story: two men and their relationship which grows out of a class divide between royalty and commoners and a cultural divide between Australia and England."

viable realistic

Guy Pearce: "I was certainly very aware of what a fascinating character I was getting to play. But I certainly didn't feel like he was necessarily the most interesting. I kind of came into the picture a little bit late, so I was probably scrambling to just make sure that I did a decent job at what I was doing."

Guy Pearce: "I was certainly ..."
http://movieline.com/2011/01/07/guy-pearce-discusses-the-kings-speech-animal-kingdom-and-filming-adam-sandler-movies/

Timothy Spall: "This isn't the chocolate-box version. There's a real emotional content, it's definitely not stiff. It's naturalistic, but written in the parlance of the time. People aren't saying, "Prime Minister, it'd be really cool if the King was replaced by his bro!"

parlance manner of speaking
bro brother

http://www.timeout.com/film/features/show-feature/11072/On_the_set_of-The_King-s_Speech-.html

Summarize why the actors were fascinated by the film, their roles or by the persons they represent in the film.

Cartoon analysis

1. What is the event or issue that inspired the cartoon?
2. Are there any real people in the cartoon? Who is portrayed? (size, facial expression, gestures …)
3. Are there symbols in the cartoon? What are they and what do they represent? Is there any text you can analyse?
4. What is the cartoonist's opinion about the topic portrayed in the cartoon? (message, effect on reader …)
5. Do you agree or disagree with the cartoonist's opinion? Why?

The King's Speech writer Seidler: "I was writing about myself"[1]

[...] It all began with screenwriter David Seidler being evacuated out of Britain to America upon an imminent Nazi attack at the brink of WWII.[1] To the then three-year-old Seidler, the treacherous trans- Atlantic ordeal was so devastating that in his subsequent childhood years after arriving in America, he had to struggle with a debilitating stammer. During the war years, he had listened on the radio to the speeches by King George VI, whom he learned was a fellow stutterer. With the King as a model, Seidler was motivated to overcome his own stammer.

The idea of telling the true story of his personal hero remained with Seidler for decades. He had been doing research on the King and found the son of his speech therapist Lionel Logue, Valentine, who had preserved his father's notes. As a loyal ex-subject, Seidler wrote to the Queen Mother requesting her approval to use her late husband's story for a movie. The following was the reply from Clarence House, the official residence of the Prince of Wales:

"Dear Mr. Seidler, thank you very much for your letter, but, please, not during my lifetime. The memory of those events is still too painful"

The Queen Mother passed away in 2002, at the age of 101. Seidler could now publicly work on a story that had captivated him all his life. But the Royal Family needs not worry. The screenplay that Seidler has written, and the film that ultimately comes out from director Tom Hooper is every bit dignified, respectful and artistically executed. What [is] more, the very human suffering and the exhilaration of overcoming an impediment are movingly told. Overall, the film is a poignant portrayal of a courageous man, a beautiful friendship, and a loving family.

Colin Firth has presented to us a reluctant hero, won us over from the start with his vulnerability and insignificance, and kept us on his side with his perseverance and loyalty. As the Queen Mother had put it, it is painful to watch him struggle to be heard. The walk to the microphone, then an advancement in technology, is as grim as the dead man walking to his execution. No wonder there is the Brahms' Requiem.

In an interview, Seidler mentions how Firth had asked him for specifics on the stuttering experience, and strived to live it in his performance. Powerful method acting indeed as Firth found himself so involved in the role that he had experienced tongue-tied episodes at public speaking. [...]

Geoffrey Rush is the crucial partner in the bromance. Without his devotion and humour, the relationship between therapist and client could not have risen to the level of trusting friendship necessary for effective treatment. It is not a cure, but the breaking down of barriers, psychological and social. Herein lies one important element of the film's success, humour. We are treated with lighthearted moments in the midst of struggles, unleashing the humanity to shine through. [...]

http://rippleeffects.wordpress.com/2011/01/06/the-kings-speech-2010/ [13 02 2013]

at the brink shortly before
treacherous *here*: dangerous
subsequent following
debilitating inhibiting
ex-subject Seidler used to live in Britain and has dual British and American citizenship
exhilaration enthusiasm
reluctant shy
perseverance persistence
bromance strong, non-sexual friendship between two men
herein there

[1] strictly speaking wrong: Seidler's family resettled later in the war.

1. What was the motivation for Seidler to write about King George VI?
2. Why did Seidler wait so long to make the film?

Think Pair Share

Are the Monarchy and the Royal Family still relevant?

1. Think:
Work on your own. List pros or cons.

2. Pair:
Work with a partner and compare your notes.

3. Share:
Meet with another pair. Two must be in favour of the Monarchy and the Royal Family and two would like the Monarchy and the Royal Family to be abolished. Discuss the question. Come to a well-founded decision.

Extra: Read one of the texts and add the arguments to your notes.

CARTOONS

SINCE WE'RE FOOTING THE BILL... GUESS WE CAN EXPECT AN INVITATION...
Royal Wedding for PRINCE WILLIAM & KATE
DAVE GRANLUND © www.davegranlund.com

EXTINCT
FORGET IT!.... ...THERE'S NO RATIONAL REASON WHY THEY'VE MADE IT INTO THE 21ST CENTURY.
UK MONARCHY
M&G 28·4·11 ZAPIRO ©

Is the monarchy still relevant?

Amy Shields: Yes

[...] Britain has had a monarchy for hundreds of years. However it has not been the same monolithic institution since it was created. Like any long-standing system, it has necessarily adapted itself to changes in the world, and therefore still remains relevant.
Recent changes have shown how the monarchy is modernising. The change in the law of succession has long been sought, with at least eleven attempts by MPs in recent years. It signals a marked break with British history, and will change the future of the monarchy forever. It means that if the Duke and Duchess of Cambridge have a daughter before a son, then she will be first in line to inherit the throne, and will remain so even if a subsequent son is born.
This in itself is a monumental change in the British monarchy, which finally brings it into line with the gender equality that is so highly valued in our modern world. The idea of overlooking females for younger and therefore less experienced male heirs is contradictory to the core beliefs of our society.
The marriage of Prince William and Kate Middleton combined the tradition of monarchy with the dawning of a new era. They have served as a reminder that there is a new generation of royals [...].
Kate also followed in the steps of Princess Diana in not vowing to 'obey' her husband. This modernisation of traditional religious vows reflects a further move towards a more accessible royal family.
The young royals are people we can all relate to. As students we can sympathise with Prince Harry in his wilder, younger days stumbling out of a nightclub. They have risked life and limb alongside the troops in Afghanistan. They associate with young people at the same universities that we ourselves attend. These are a generation with the same life experiences as us, and no longer the distant elite that they used to be.
Our monarchy is part of what defines us as British. They are an instantly recognisable image of our country across the world. Our current monarch is approaching her 60th year on the throne. Whilst the Prime Minister and the government are the fundamental machinery of running the country, the monarchy is the face of Britain that is remembered.
Clearly the monarchy still reaches out to people. [...] It has been suggested that as many as 24 million people tuned in to watch the wedding of William and Kate. Clearly there is still an emotional investment by the British people in the royal family.
To abolish the Royal Family would be to discount centuries of history and tradition. The monarchy is an institution that Britain should be proud to claim. They offer us a link with our history and I for one think it would be a royal shame to abandon that.

monolithic *aus einem Guss*

law of succession *Gesetz der Erbfolge*
MP = Member of Parliament

heir *here:* the next person to be King or Queen

dawning beginning

to vow to promise

Amy Shields: Yes:
http://thecourieronline.co.uk/2011/11/is-the-monarchy-still-relevant-in-modern-society/ [07 12 2012]

List Shields's arguments in favour of monarchy.

Is the monarchy still relevant?

Ralph Blackburn: No

The recent legislation regarding the monarchy outlines the precise problem with the Royal Family in the modern age. With plaudits being piled upon the law, stating that a daughter will become monarch even if a son is born, is averting from the fact that it has taken up until 2011 to end old fashioned sexism being enshrined in law; This being the first time since 1772 that the Royal Marriages Act has been changed.

Over the past century, universal suffrage has come into place and hereditary peers have been abolished from the House of Lords, yet the monarchy is still holding Britain back from becoming a truly modern state.

It represents classism, inequality and prejudice; Roman Catholics, whilst now being able to marry into the Royal Family, can still not become monarchs, due to Henry VIII's schism of just under 500 years ago, based entirely on personal preference.

The modern multicultural state of Britain has no place for implicit religious prejudice. These issues which have largely been solved in the recent parliament act, are not even the main problems with the monarchy in the modern age.

Unelected officials, with prerogative powers have no place in a modern democracy. In the latest election, there was confusion as to who should form the government, with the Queen possibly having the decisive outcome on which party would form a coalition with the Liberal Democrats.

The economic benefits and deficiencies of the Royal Family are fairly even, with the amount the taxpayer pays towards the Royal Family, clearly accounted through the civil list. The civil list is the annual grant from parliament towards the monarchy for official functions. From 2010 – 2011, parliament paid £14.5m towards the monarchy which is approximately 68p per taxpayer. That's roughly doubled over 2011 due to £20m spent on the police presence for the Royal wedding, although effectively cancelled out due to increase in tourism revenue. 68p may not seem a large amount, however when tuitions fees have risen to £9,000, the NHS is being cut and EMA has been scrapped, paying £14.5m towards an outdated system seems absolutely ridiculous.

Given the vast inherited fortune which the Royal Family possess, by 2011 they surely can at least be self sufficient. Whilst over the course of the 20th century there were a variety of roles for the Royal Family regarding the Commonwealth, over the past 10 years they have been transformed into a laughing stock by the tabloid press. Prince Harry staggering out of clubs dressed as a Nazi does nothing to alleviate the public perception. The two Princes have done minimal official appearances over the past few years, Prince William averaging a fairly measly 14 per year. On average over the 1980s Prince Charles fulfilled 84 official appearances whereas Princess Diana over 100. Clearly over the past 25 years the official role of the monarchy has decreased whilst the cost has increased. We should live in an egalitarian state, not one still influenced by such a high standing background

plaudits public expression of approval

suffrage the right to vote

schism *here:* breaking with Rome

prerogative birthright

tuition instruction
NHS National Health Service
EMA European Medicines Agency

Ralph Blackburn: No:
http://thecourieronline.co.uk/2011/11/is-the-monarchy-still-relevant-in-modern-society [07 12 2012]

List Blackburn's arguments against monarchy.

Bildnachweis

S. 3, 5: Weinstein Co.; S. 51 (beide): Matthias Berghahn/Verlagsarchiv Schöningh; S. 58: Franz-Josef Domke/Verlagsarchiv Schöningh; S. 84/88/89 (jew. beide), S. 119, S. 120: © Kobal collection; S. 60 oben: Livernois, via Wikimedia Commons; S. 60 unten: picture-alliance/akg-images; S. 61: Matson Photo Service, via Wikimedia Commons; S. 63/S. 125, S. 65 1.–3. Abb.: picture alliance/dpa; S. 64 1. Abb., S. 102: © Allan Warren; 2. Abb.: Photo: Mr. Clemens via Wikimedia Commons; 3. Abb.: Allan warren (Own work) [CC-BY-SA-3.0 (http://creativecommons.org/licenses/by-sa/3.0) or GFDL (http://www.gnu.org/copyleft/fdl.html)], via Wikimedia Commons; 4. Abb.: picture alliance/empics; 5. Abb.: John Pannell (Flickr: DSC_0760) [CC-BY-2.0 (http://creativecommons.org/licenses/by/2.0)], via Wikimedia Commons; S. 65 4. Abb.: picture alliance/ZUMAPRESS.com; S. 101: http://en.wikipedia.org/wiki/File:Duke_and_Duchess_of_Windsor_meet_Adolf_Hitler_1937.jpg; S. 115f.: Logue family archive; S. 123: www.CartoonStock.com; S. 126 oben: © David Granlund; S. 126 unten: © 2010–2012 Zapiro / www.zapiro.com (All Rights Reserved)

Sollte trotz aller Bemühungen um korrekte Urheberangaben ein Irrtum unterlaufen sein, bitten wir darum, sich mit dem Verlag in Verbindung zu setzen, damit wir eventuell erforderliche Korrekturen vornehmen können.

EinFach Englisch
Unterrichtsmodelle

Herausgegeben von Hans Kröger in Zusammenarbeit mit Carmen Mendez

Ausgewählte Titel der Reihe:

Cultures in Conflict?
Literature on Ethnic Relationships
115 S., DIN A4, kart. Best.-Nr. 041220
Audio-CD: 74 Min. Best.-Nr. 062407
Textausgabe: 148 S. Best.-Nr. 041218

Echoes of the Empire.
The Mixed Voices of a Colonial Past
20th Century English Short Stories
119 S., DIN A4, kart. Best.-Nr. 041223
Audio-CD: 78 Min. Best.-Nr. 062405
Textausgabe: 168 S. Best.-Nr. 041224

Political Speeches
Historical & Topical Issues
127 S., DIN A4, kart. Best.-Nr. 041236
Audio-CD: 70 Min. Best.-Nr. 062409
Textausgabe: 132 S. Best.-Nr. 041234

Utopia and Dystopia
Exploring Alternative Worlds
92 S., DIN A4, kart. Best.-Nr. 041204
Textausgabe: 92 S. Best.-Nr. 041202

Bend it Like Beckham
Filmanalyse
86 S., DIN A4, geh. Best.-Nr. 041212

Dead Poets Society
Filmanalyse
67 S., DIN A4, geh. Best.-Nr. 041255

East is East
Filmanalyse
101 S., DIN A4, kart. Best.-Nr. 041228

Four Weddings and a Funeral
Filmanalyse
115 S., DIN A4, kart. Best.-Nr. 041178

An Inconvenient Truth
Filmanalyse
91 S., DIN A4, kart. Best.-Nr. 041186

Outsourced
Filmanalyse
110 S., DIN A4, kart. Best.-Nr. 041172

Slumdog Millionaire
Filmanalyse
90 S., DIN A4, kart. Best.-Nr. 041189

Don DeLillo: Falling Man
99 S., DIN A4, kart. Best.-Nr. 041181

Mark Haddon: The Curious Incident of the Dog in the Night-Time
99 S., DIN A4, kart. Best.-Nr. 041252

Mohsin Hamid: The Reluctant Fundamentalist
92 S., DIN A4, kart. Best.-Nr. 041171

Lorraine Hansberry: A Raisin in the Sun
98 S., DIN A4, kart. Best.-Nr. 041241

Nick Hornby: About a Boy
inkl. Filmanalyse
93 S., DIN A4, kart. Best.-Nr. 041245

Nick Hornby: Slam
123 S., DIN A4, kart. Best.-Nr. 041248

Aldous Huxley: Brave New World
93 S., DIN A4, kart. Best.-Nr. 041249

Hanif Kureishi: The Black Album
114 S., DIN A4, kart. Best.-Nr. 041179

Nick McDonell: Twelve
100 S., DIN A4, kart. Best.-Nr. 041194

Robert Swindells: Daz 4 Zoe
91 S., DIN A4, kart. Best.-Nr. 041170

Tennessee Williams: A Streetcar Named Desire
102 S., DIN A4, kart. Best.-Nr. 041238